HOW TO WRITE A BOOK

HOW TO WRITE A BOOK

✧

Dennis Jernigan

innovo
PUBLISHING

Innovo Publishing LLC
www.innovopublishing.com
1-888-546-2111

Innovo
PUBLISHING

Providing Full-Service Publishing Services for
Christian Authors, Artists, and Ministries: Hardbacks, Paperbacks,
eBooks, Audiobooks, Music, and Film

HOW TO WRITE A BOOK

The masculine singular pronoun (he/him/his) is used throughout this book to
indicate either gender.

Library of Congress Control Number: 2015953071
ISBN 13: 978-1-61314-299-8

Interior Layout & Cover Design by Innovo Publishing LLC
and Eternity Communications

Printed in the United States of America
U.S. Printing History

First Edition: October 2015

This book is dedicated to all those would-be writers who have books within them just waiting to be written.

To all those who have been told they can't.

To all those who've been told they have nothing to say.

*This book is also dedicated to my wife, Melinda;
my children; my grandchildren;
and to the generations in my family to come.*

Acknowledgments

I need only look as far as my relationship with my wife, my children, my grandchildren, my friends, and—most importantly—my God to be filled with inspiration to write. The possibilities are, indeed, endless.

Table of Contents

"I have been successful probably because I have already realized that I knew nothing about writing and have merely tried to tell an interesting story entertainingly."
— Edgar Rice Burroughs

Preface

What makes me an expert on writing books? Nothing really, other than the fact that I have written, to date, twenty books. Two are autobiographical in nature. Some are self-help books. Many are Christian devotional books. And three are fantasy novels for young people. Three of my books have gone on to sell in excess of twelve thousand copies each. The others continue to sell hundreds of copies each year. Ten have been published (including this one) by traditional publishing houses. Eleven have been self-published.

In college, I trained as a musician but was told I had no potential as a songwriter, so I was not allowed to major in songwriting. For four years I slogged through music classes dreaming of writing a song, being told that was someone else's gift and someone else's dream. After college, I began to write songs anyway. To date, I've had over five hundred published. Go figure. The reality that I had allowed what some "expert" thought of me determine my pursuit of a dream changed my entire attitude. From that point on, my attitude was: "Don't tell me I can't do something I've dreamt of doing. I'll pursue my dreams!"

I am no expert, but I have sold a few books in both the traditional publishing and self-publishing realm. Neither would have happened had I never taken the time to write a book! I dreamed of writing a book "someday." At one point in my life, I came to the conclusion that I could either wait around for a publishing deal or I could go ahead and begin writing just in case "someday" ever came along. In other words, I followed my dream rather than waiting for the dream to happen! In the late 1990s, I dreamed of writing a book. So I did. And suddenly a publisher asked me to write a book on something that I had just written! That first book even won a national award! My point? If I had never written the book, none of that would have been possible.

The goal of this book is not to get you "published," but rather, to help you create something *to* publish! Think about this: every author who has ever been published was once an *un*published author! I want you to feel emboldened and empowered to step out and write your book by the time you reach the last word of *this* book!

You and I live in a day and age where the impossible is possible. ANYONE can publish a book using today's wonderful technology. But nothing gets published if nothing gets written. The purpose of this book is to give you the simple nuts and bolts I use when writing a book. Take what you need. Chuck the rest. My desire is to see you not only dream the dream—but WRITE the dream! Read on and I'll let you in on some of my "secrets."

Dennis Jernigan

"If you have other things in your life—family, friend, good productive day work—these can interact with your writing and the sum will be all the richer."
— David Brin

CHAPTER ONE

✧

WHY WRITE A BOOK ON HOW TO WRITE A BOOK?

"Any man who keeps working is not a failure. He may not be a great writer, but if he applies the old-fashioned virtues of hard, constant labor, he'll eventually make some kind of career for himself as writer."

— Ray Bradbury

Why write a book on how to write a book?

For me, the answer is quite simple. I do not want people to have to go through the unnecessary delay of seeing their dreams come to fruition when the simple steps to bringing about those very dreams are much simpler than they try to make them.

I wrote this book because I felt I had something—some things—to say that might influence or enhance someone else's life in a positive way. Having grown sick and tired of being sick and tired of never putting pen to paper, I got off my duff one day and said to myself, "It's time to stop talking about writing a book and time to start writing that book!"

When I first set out to write that first book, I did not have the luxury of the Internet. There were no laptops I could afford. An iPhone? Are you kidding me? I began writing books in the late 1990s. At first, I wrote in longhand, using that most antiquated media form of pen and paper. That soon grew tedious enough for me that I sought out other forms of newfangled writing tools. The job I held at the time afforded me access to one of the early Macs. The trusty old SE model! After simply asking if I could use the Mac for personal writing, I was granted the permission I needed—so I began writing!

Talk about liberating! Who knew that simply taking the first step to writing a book—actually committing words to paper—would free me to unleash the passion that had been burning in me. I know it sounds ridiculous, but writing helped free me up to write! Even though I was a young man in my late thirties, I felt I had lived a sufficient amount of time and had experienced a lifetime's worth of adventures. Through the process of living said life, I had come to a place of wisdom that I thought could benefit others.

I already knew what I wanted to write about. In fact, I felt I had a plethora of information. Too much information. In order to give myself direction and to help weed out the unnecessary information, I wrote a simple outline. At that time I began calling my outline my road map—because it guided me to my intended destination and helped me stay on track for the journey!

I believe everyone has a story to tell. Everyone. Not every person has the same story as the next. Not every person talks in the same manner. Not every person will write a personal story. Not every person will write fiction. But it is my firm belief that the lives we live will shape whatever style of story or book we plan to write. My life helps shape my self-help books. My life helps shape the fantasy books I write. My life is a treasure trove rich and deep in adventure that will serve me well to the end of my writing days. And so is yours!

And I want that for you. Are you ready to write?

CHAPTER TWO

✧

WHERE DO I BEGIN?

"If you ask me what I came into this world to do, I will tell you: I came to live out loud."
— Emile Zola

"Master your instrument, master the music, and then forget all that . . . and just play."
— Charlie Parker, Jazz great

"The only thing that stands between a man and what he wants from life is often merely the will to try it and the faith to believe that it is possible."
—Richard M. DeVos

"No journey begins without the first step."
—Dennis Jernigan

A Spanish proverb says, *"If you build no castles in the air, you build no castles anywhere."*

We can talk about taking the journey all we want, but unless we take that very first step, we will get absolutely nowhere. We can dream about writing a book—building a most fabulous castle in the air of our dreams—and build nothing toward which we labored! We can set ourselves up to succeed as easily as we set ourselves up to fail. If we make no preparations for the journey—for the writing of the book we dream of writing—we will get nothing done. Let me ask you a few simple questions.

- Do you have an idea for the book you wish to write?
- What day are you going to actually begin writing?
- When is the deadline for completing your book?
- Do you have a laptop or personal computer?
- Do you have something—writing software—on which to write that book?
- Do you have an iPad or tablet device of some kind?
- Do you at least have a pencil and paper?

If you have a simple idea and a means of writing it down, you are already prepared to take your first step! I know. I know. This sounds like oversimplification—and it is, in a way. I just wanted you to see that you may be further down the road than you even realize! If you have inspiration and something with which to write, you're almost there!

What is inspiration? According to most dictionaries, inspiration is "stimulation of the mind or feelings that serve as a catalyst to creativity." According to the Greek translation of the word *inspired* in the Bible, specifically the New Testament, to be inspired means to have an idea "God-breathed" into one's mind. Regardless of what you believe about inspiration, without inspiration one has no ideas. Without ideas, one has nowhere to go. Without a place—or story—to write, you have nothing. More specifically, what is *your* inspiration? Do you wish to write a book just to say you've written a book? That doesn't sound very interesting at all!

So where, exactly, do you begin? Think about the quote I wrote at the head of this chapter: "No journey begins without the first step." If you never put pen to paper—or fingers to keyboard—you get absolutely NOWHERE. Following are some key questions that will help you determine exactly where you are in the process of writing your book. And, after all, asking the "right/write" questions is vital to helping you take that very first step.

What Is My Subject?

Knowing you want to write a book and having something to write about are two different things. How can you get to where you're going if you do not know where you wish to go? Just sayin'!

Who Is My Target Audience?

Who is most likely to read a book about the subject matter you are addressing? Whether you like it or not, most writing is to a niche—very specific and often small—audience. We all want to write that "million-seller," but it is the niche author who proves to be most successful. What is my target audience for this book? Would-be writers and or authors! Write to those you are trying to reach, and do not be so concerned about trying to cover each and every base of each and everything you wish to eventually say throughout the course of your writing career.

Do you think Tom Clancy was trying to reach the female love-story crowd, or was he trying to reach those who enjoy a great thriller? Do you think Stephen King was going after the kid-lit crowd, ages five to ten, or was he seeking readers who enjoy horror and suspense? Do you think Erica Jong was trying to sell to the adult male audience, ages thirty to forty-five, or was she trying to reach the female crowd who love a great sexually charged love story? My point? Know your audience and write to IT!

What Needs Could I Address?

Are you writing a self-help book? A how-to book? Then be specific to that audience. This book is a self-help book. My hope is to make it as informative and as simple as possible without boring you out of your mind. To quote the old TV series *Dragnet*: "Just the facts, ma'am."

If I Were Looking for This Type of Book, What Would I Want to Know?

When I read a self-help/how-to book, I want simplicity and I want my questions answered. Counselors, by and large, will tell you that meeting the emotional needs of their clients often boils down to asking the right questions. Are you going to write a fantasy-thriller? Then what does that group love to read when they pick up a fantasy-thriller? Are you going to write a romance novel? What does that genre love to have included in such a book? Are you going to write your autobiography? What are the things you would want to know about someone else if you were reading another person's autobiography? Knowing the right questions to ask will help you with the most helpful aspect of writing your book—the outline. We'll deal with how to write an inspiration-inducing outline in the next chapter.

What Is My Deadline for Completing This Project?

If you want to write a book, my personal belief is that you should give yourself realistic deadlines and goals. My deadline for writing this book you are now reading was four weeks! I know that sounds ridiculous, but I am a very motivated person, and I know that my personality type works best when given deadlines—or under pressure! I began writing the book on April 4 and my goal was to have the entire book ready for editing by April 30! Giving myself deadlines also causes me to streamline my words, helping me avoid verbosity. Setting realistic goals for myself also helps me with creating the best possible outline or road map from which to write.

How Many Chapters Per Week/Per Day Would I Need to Write to Achieve This Goal?

Once you've written your outline (discussed in the next chapter), you will have a much better grasp on setting realistic goals for your writing schedule. Once I have written and streamlined my outline, I know exactly where I need to go and what routes I'll need to take to arrive at my final destination. When I can gain a clear picture of where I am headed, I have a much better grasp on exactly how long it might take me to get there. For some, this goal may be to write one chapter per week. Perhaps you only have time to write one chapter per month. Whatever your reality is, adapt your schedule to reflect these realities and set your pace accordingly. When I am in book-writing-mode, my personal goal is a chapter a day during the work week. While I am not always able to maintain that schedule, I stay as close to it as possible, writing early in the day. This leaves me time in the afternoon to focus on less brain-muscle-requiring activities! Often, if you're anything like I am, you'll discover that once you are on a roll in full writing mode, you will be able to write more than one chapter in a day. Personally, I'm not an "I've got to write 10,000–15,000 words-a-day" kind of guy. My personal reality is that I like to capture complete thoughts rather than a certain number of words. This works best for me. As you begin to write, you will discover what works best for you.

How Long Should the Book Be?

Again, you have to know where you're going and how you want to get there to know the answer to this question. Have I already mentioned how important your outline (road map) is? I cannot stress this point enough. Your outline is a major factor in the completion of your book. And, again, we will discuss this in detail in the next chapter.

How Do I Find Time to Write?

We tend to make time for what is a priority in our lives. If you have time to play a round of golf (or two) each week, you have time to write. If you have time to have tea with the ladies a couple of times each week, you have time to write. In other words, you'll find out quickly what your priorities are by taking an honest look at what you spend your time doing.

When I began writing, my wife and I had nine children—on purpose! I worked full time and then helped with the children when not working. My vision to write my first book had to fit within my priorities—and had to become a priority if I was to carve out time to actually write. My priorities are this: God, wife, children, job, friends, and writing. In order for me to actually find the time to write, I had to determine what time I could take away from my realistic priorities without bringing harm. Practically, the first place I could carve time from was my recreational activities. I could cut out a tennis outing with a buddy to write, but I was not willing to take time away from my children. I would urge you to simply make an honest list of the priorities of your own life and then decide what you can take time away from in order to write.

Writing can be done in five-minutes-at-a-time increments. Writing can be done in time slots of an hour. Writing can be done after the kids go to bed. Writing can be done by waking earlier than everyone else. My point is this: You will make time for what is important to you, and if writing is important, you *can* make time for it. My only proviso is this: do not take time away from a priority if it will bring harm. Are you willing to make sacrifices that take away from your own comfort, or is personal comfort more important than your vision to write a book? Just asking.

Once you have taken a realistic look at your personal schedule, set aside a daily or every other day or weekly time to write—and then use it for WRITING! Don't write out your grocery list or make a new client list. Write. Even if all you have is five minutes, use that five minutes and WRITE. Five minutes are better than zero minutes as far as I am able to discern. And accomplishing a small goal—like writing for five minutes a day—will give you a sense of accomplishment and actually serve as a catalyst to even more writing in those five-minute bursts of prose! Your own attitude makes the difference between getting words on paper or doing nothing at all.

Even as I write these words, my wife and I are in Australia visiting our daughter and son-in-law and our first granddaughter. Time is precious to me. So, when the baby goes to sleep and everyone else is napping, I am writing while I have quiet time in the house, even though my body and mind are crying out for a nap of their own! Bringing a book to life requires sacrifice on my part. What sacrifices are you willing to make in order to see your book come to fruition?

Perhaps the next chapter will give you that extra little push you've been needing. Why do I say that? Because once I know where I am going and how I am going to get there, I am unstoppable in my passion and single-mindedness in getting there. Read on to find out how to build *your* road map to completing your book.

CHAPTER THREE

✧

THE ROAD MAP

"Having no plan is like leaping off a precipice and trying to knit yourself a parachute on the way down."
— Kelli Jae Baeli, Armchair Detective

"Give me six hours to chop down a tree and I will spend the first four sharpening the axe."
— Abraham Lincoln

Just as with the saying that no journey begins without the first step, no journey is ever completed if one does not even now where he is going. And think about the quotes above. Who in his right mind would jump off a cliff with no parachute, hoping to build one on the way down? And why waste six hours of time trying to chop down a tree with a dull axe when the time it would take to sharpen said axe would lessen the amount of energy one would have wasted otherwise? Planning is the key to success when writing a book, even if that plan is rudimentary.

When I wrote my first book, I knew exactly what I wanted to say, but I did not necessarily know just how in the world I would ever get there—until someone suggested I write an outline. Even though I knew exactly where I wanted to go, I had not taken the time to map out just how I was going to get there. But I'll tell you this: once I began to write my outline, the passion that simple task unleashed in my soul sent me on a tear to begin writing with gusto! And write I did. I finished that book in one month's time simply because I had a plan—and stuck to it—for the most part!

I am about to tell you one of my best-kept secrets about the way I approach writing. Even though I have a definite course set, I never limit myself to staying rigidly on that path. What joy is a journey if we do not take the time to go off the beaten path for a few minutes—do some exploring? I find that the road map, once I have begun my journey, actually lends itself to sending me and my heart on little side trips that translate to the heart of my subject—such as adding just the right amount of spice to create a tasty stew is the permission I allow myself to go off the path from time to time. The key to building a stew (and writing a book) is not going overboard with the spice—or not adding enough to begin with—as long as we eventually find our way back to the course set before us.

One of the best things I have learned about writing a book is simply to write what I know. At least that is what I have learned when writing my self-help/how-to books. Since I know a bit about how to write and publish a book, I thought perhaps I would write from the experience I have had in my own learning process. I am simply writing what I know in the hope that it may encourage others to step out of their own comfort zones and actually DO what is burning in their hearts to do concerning writing their own books.

But even when it comes to my fantasy writing, I tend to write what I know. It's called imagination, one of the greatest gifts given to mankind. Even though I have not visited many exotic lands, the contrary is true in my dream life. Imagination—much like creativity—is learning to see life from a different point of view.

When I was a boy, I went through many traumatic times—a lot of hurt and hidden pain. My only refuge at times was my ability to dream. As soon as my head would hit the pillow, I was no longer a farm boy in rural Oklahoma. The instant I went to sleep I found myself suddenly transported to the *USS Enterprise*, my dad none other than Captain James Tiberius Kirk! The recurring adventures I experienced each night centered around my being captured and wounded (much as in my conscious life) by whatever the latest race of alien and sinister life-form my mind could conjure up. Just as said alien life-form was about to put me to death, my dad would materialize with his phaser set not to "stun" but to "destroy"—and the aliens would be dispatched summarily. And I would wake up just at that moment as my mother in my dreams (Doris Day) sang the sweet refrain, "Que sera, sera, \ whatever will be, will be, \ the future's not ours to see, \ que sera, sera."

As I soon discovered in my dreams that I could will myself to dream vast and wonderful adventures in my sleep, I discovered that I could do the same when writing. Yes, I follow the road map, but sometimes the little side road I see along the way may just lead me to a view of Oz! Write what you know— and you probably know more than you think you do!

Now, about that road map I keep mentioning. The best way to show you why I'm spending so much time talking about the destination is to give you an example. Following is the outline I wrote for this book. It took me less than an hour to write down what I consider the meatiest of the subject matter I would want someone to have told me when I was first starting out as a writer. You will notice that I have stuck to the road map by and large but have taken several little side trips to help illustrate the absolute joy that is virtually guaranteed when you have a map to follow.

The outline allows me to see all the way from the first step of my journey to the final destination—and in the process, gives me an overall big-picture mentality in which I am able to step back and see the little side trips I want to take along the way. This simply builds my anticipation in wanting to get to those little stepping-off places and keeps me intensely focused on the daily goals I set myself for wiring.

The outline also keeps me focused on the road ahead. Have you ever tried to drive a vehicle while staring in the rearview mirror? It's virtually impossible to do—at least very well! The road map frees me up from the fear of wondering if I forgot to mention something earlier and actually gives me peace in knowing that, according to my map, I've already covered that ground so there is no need to go back! A writer can keep his eyes firmly gazing on the road ahead when he is following his map. The only use for the rearview mirror is to help one gain his bearings—but never for major navigation!

The outline is your injection of actually taking what inspired you in the first place and, like a wonder drug, fills your heart with freedom and passion and peace in knowing that you are well within the bounds of your creativity—and free to fly wherever that map takes you! Having raised nine children, my wife and I learned early on that in order to keep our children focused on a good path toward being responsible adults, we needed to place boundaries upon their lives. They learned quickly that boundaries are not meant to stifle or suppress but rather to nurture and protect. Boundaries keep children from danger and trouble. Your outline—your road map—is designed to do the same. Follow your map and you won't lack for creativity within its bounds—and your book will be the better for it.

I would like to express one more thing about having and following your outline. I am sure you have heard people talk about having writer's block. Honestly, I have never come up against such a thing. When I have created my outline, I have given my heart something to hope for and my mind something to think on. How many times have you heard of a person retiring only to pass away within weeks or even days of said retirement? Part of the reason for that phenomenon is the fact that the human heart needs something to live for. The human mind needs something to engage it—or the heart and mind will lose hope. Writing my outline gives me something to hope in and think about and essentially live for during that particular season. It is one of the healthiest things I can do for my mind.

Have I made my point yet? I think I have! Once I created the following outline, I began planning a time to begin writing. Two days after I made my map I found myself having a sleepless night here in Australia. Rather than pout about not being able to sleep, I decided I would use the time I was awake to begin writing my book about writing a book. Basically, I practiced what I preach! My goal was to write until sleepiness set in, but I found myself completing the entire preface and first chapter and then beginning to write the third chapter! Why? Because I had a road map to follow and a destination to get to—and I had hope filling my heart because I knew I was on to something that would help a lot of other people!

Here is my outline in its original form. Notice the variations—side trips—I have already made, and we're only on chapter three! Study what I've written and pattern your own outline after, if you wish. Writing my outline actually freed my mind from worrying about whether I left something out or not. You can free your mind right now. After you read my outline for this book, sit down—right now—and write *your* outline for *your* book!

How to Write a Book—Outline

Preface

I. **Why write a book on how to write a book?**
 A. My publishing history and why I wrote my first book
 B. My passion to share what I knew
 C. Everybody has a story to tell

II. **Where do I begin?**
 A. Inspiration—No journey begins without the first step
 B. Asking the "right/write" questions
  1. What is my subject?
  2. Who is my target audience?
  3. What needs could I address?
  4. If I were looking for this type of book, what would I want to know?
  5. What is my deadline for completing this project?
  6. How many chapters per week/per day would I need to write to achieve this goal?
  7. How long should the book be? Refer to your road map.
 C. Finding/Making time to write
  1. Dedicated writing time
  2. Five minutes is better than zero-minutes attitude
 D. Beginning—write something—even if it is one paragraph

III. **Write what you know—writing tools**
 A. Content is king
 B. How to write an outline—the road map
  1. Do not be afraid to take side trips
 C. What if I do not have the gift of prose?
  1. Ghostwriting for those who lack the gift of prose
  2. Find a friend/associate who has the gift
  3. Make digital voice recordings or dictate to yourself

D. Back up your work daily!
   1. Hard copy
   2. E-mail each day's work to yourself
   3. Send a copy to a trusted friend or associate

IV. **Editing**
   A. Self-editing
   B. Trusted friends
   C. Accountability—those pesky goals and deadlines
   D. Editing one chapter at a time vs. editing the entire book
   E. How to find a professional editor—or that English teacher friend
   F. Copyrighting your work

V. **Formatting your book**
   A. The eBook is your friend
   B. Kindle, Nook, ePub, iPad, etc.
   C. How to format your book as an eBook

VI. **The advent of self-publishing and eBooks**
   A. The statistics
   B. Self-publishing vs. traditional publishing
   C. Marketing one's own works—using the Web

VII. **Marketing your book**
   A. Create a website
   B. Join Facebook
   C. Write a blog
   D. Utilize family, friends, and associates
   E. Utilize YouTube
   F. Online author/writing groups
   G. Equip yourself for the job

VIII. **Pricing and distribution**
   A. The eBook is your friend
   B. Should I print books?
      1. Print-on-demand

IX. Don't apologize for a dream
   A. You'll never know if you never try
   B. Don't cast your pearls before swine

X. Arrive at your destination
   A. Reiterate your goal
   B. Encourage and cast vision
   C. End with a satisfying conclusion or leave them wanting MORE!

CHAPTER FOUR

✧

THE TOOLS OF THE TRADE

"If you don't have the time to read, you don't have the time (or the tools) to write."
— Stephen King

"Do not wait; the time will never be 'just right.' Start where you stand, and work with whatever tools you may have at your command, and better tools will be found as you go along."
— George Herbert

"One of the greatest and simplest tools for learning more and growing is doing more"
—Washington Irving

A quote I've heard several times through the years concerning writing a book is "Content is king." In other words, what is *in* your book—what your final destination is and how you get there—is of vital importance. Yet, that content must be matched with a niche that needs and wants that content. Knowing this begs the question, "Then how do I know that what I want to write will be the 'right' thing about which to write?" The answer is in the inspiration. Remember, we write what we know, and we know more than we think we do. If we approach writing a book as we would a much-anticipated project or activity or, dare I say, job, what is vital to getting that project done or enjoying the activity with ease and doing a job that leaves us feeling fulfilled? Using the right tools for said project, activity, or job.

Let's take a quick inventory of the tools already at your disposal. You have an idea. That tells us you have a mind. You have the physical ability to put pen to paper—or finger to keyboard—as it were. You have the time for other things you enjoy besides writing. You have a written outline, right? These are the simplest yet most important tools you have—just waiting to be used!

This is where so many people I have talked with through the years—people who stop me and ask me "How did you get your start in writing?" or "How do I write a book?"—get stuck. They have everything they need to begin, but they allow one little thing to become a huge roadblock to actually writing a book. What is that? When someone asks me those questions, I simply tell them, "I simply began to write," at which point they say, "But I've never written before. I don't know what to do!" And to that I simply say, "Then you need to start writing." Usually a lightbulb turns on in their minds as they begin to process the simplicity of that statement.

When people ask me how to write a book and I tell them to just start writing the book, there are sometimes individuals who look at me with such bewilderment and confusion that I know the real question they want to ask but are too afraid to pose is, "How do I get my book published?" If that is the real case, then they are getting the cart before the horse and, in my humble opinion, probably have no idea of what they want to write about or that they are so insecure in their identity. This tells me their hope is that people will like them and that if they can just write a book, then they will be somebody of significance. To these groups I say, "Write your book because of the passion that burns in your heart whether you get it published or not (and ANYONE can get a book published these days—more on that later). Write your book whether people like you or not—simply because you are passionate about what you are writing about. Write as if you really believe people out there need what you have to say."

> *"Procrastination is the art of keeping up with yesterday."*
> —Don Marquis

> *"Procrastination makes easy things hard, hard things harder."*
> —Mason Cooley

> *"Procrastination is opportunity's assassin."*
> —Victor Kiam

> *"Procrastination is the thief of time."*
> —Edward Young

In case you're wondering, I believe there is one major roadblock to writing your book that is insidious in nature. Procrastination—putting off doing something until a later time. What are the reasons we procrastinate? Often, we simply do not want to put out the effort—especially if that thing we are putting off requires work, gets us out of our comfort zone, or is simply tedious. We have already discussed what I believe about finding the time to write. We make time for that which we truly see as a priority. So my next question involves that reality. Do you really want to write or is it simply a pipe dream?

A vain imagination? Too tedious? Here's a greater reality: your book is not going to write itself! Get off your duff and "man up" (or "woman up"), as we say here in Oklahoma, and simply begin writing!

I guarantee you this: once you begin writing, you will feel a release of endorphins and an emotional lift as you would when taking the first step of a much-anticipated journey. I guarantee the more you write, the more you'll be inspired; and the more you write, the more tools you will pick up along the way. Do not put off writing any longer. To keep coming up with excuses is playing right into procrastination's hands. Your time is robbed. Your dreams are continually crushed. Eventually, years will have gone by and your heart will fill with regret—and then you die, having never accomplished the simplest of dreams to fulfill. You never wrote one word because the "time was never right" or you had "other things that needed to be done before you could ever begin writing."

Let me ask you one more question. When you get to the end of your life, what would you regret not having ever at least tried? If writing your story—your book—is one of those regrets now, don't you think it might be a regret then? Right now you have the tools to do something about that. I know your mind is probably coming up with other excuses like "but I don't have the necessary tools to write" or "I don't even know what my writing voice (style) should be" and other such questions. Let me set your mind at ease. You already have the tools you need and your voice—your particular style—is already in place. It just needs to be given the proper platform on which to stand. And you've got that too!

As I was growing up, we did not have much—but we were happy. Not having much financial resource was of little consequence to a hard-working farm family such as ours. We were resourceful. We learned to use the tools we had rather than to sit around dreaming about the tools we didn't have. I can recall my dad grinding flour from the wheat we had grown so my mom could bake bread. Personally, I remember getting up each morning and milking the cows so we would have milk to drink and extra to sell to the neighbors. We used what we had and thrived as a result.

After I was married, one of my first jobs entailed working for an organization as a secretary in the morning and as a janitor in the afternoon. During that time, I was asked if I could come up with designs for a series of banners for the organization to display. They had no budget for actual design artists, and they had no money for anything more than basic materials. When ideas confront necessity but there are no financial resources, creativity begins to truly kick in.

We found a roll of unused butcher paper in the basement, and I bought a can of gold metallic paint and two beveled foam paint brushes. And using my calligraphy skills, I wrote the desired words on the paper. Once hung from simple frames made of inexpensive wooden slats, the distance from the viewers' eyes to the banners gave the appearance of something remarkable. People would walk into the main hall where the banners were hung and be awestruck, often asking me if the banner was cloth or satin. On one such occasion, I told the person to reach up and touch the bottom of the banner. Much to my delight, they exclaimed, "It's PAPER!" We used what we had and coupled that with the resources of our own talents and abilities, and the result was something quite pleasing to the eye. We used what we had.

When I began writing music, I had no budget for recording that music. After a few weeks I was able to save enough money to purchase a Tascam four-track cassette recorder. I recorded a simple twelve-song, less-than-demo-quality album with the simple dream of sharing the songs with friends. One year after recording that simple tape we had sold over sixty thousand units using—you guessed it—what we had at the time.

To share any more stories would belabor the point. Let's make a list of all the tools you have right now. Ready?

Tools You Have Right Now

- Idea for your book
- The ability to type
- Scheduled time to write
- Outline
- Something to either write on or type on
- The ability to physically put pen to paper or type on a keyboard

Let me add one more item to the list of tools you have at your disposal right now. You have your voice or style already *in* you—you've just never released it until now! My favorite way of writing is to write the way in which I naturally talk or convey ideas to someone else. My favorite books to read are books in which I can tell the author is writing to me just as he would talk to me. It reads in a very natural and well-conveyed sense to my mind. I know not everyone enjoys the same style of writing, but I have learned to enjoy almost any type of writing. How? By reading different styles!

You will never know your particular style or voice until you actually write. When I write self-help books, I tend to be more cut and dried in my style. When I write a fantasy novel, I tend to be much more narrative and emotional in my style. When I write in an autobiographical voice, I tend to be almost too honest—to the point of people telling me they actually felt what I was feeling as I wrote. And in each case, I write from my own voice because it is *my* voice. Think about this: no one has your particular voice because there is not another you. You have a story to tell that no one else can tell. You have things to say in your own way that nobody else can adequately say. You have the most amazing tool—like a lion that has been caged too long and longs for that moment of release when it can run wild in the realm in which it was intended to run free all along. Release your voice. How? By WRITING!

Here's your next list of tools you will possibly need to help you in your writing:

Tools You Need to Have

- Computer, laptop, iPad, etc.
- Writing software
- Dictionary
- Thesaurus
- Digital voice recorder
- Access to the Internet
- Trusted friends and associates off whom to bounce ideas
- Hard drive for backing up your work

If you do not have a computer or writing software, get creative. Use paper and pen. Ask to borrow time on a friend's computer. Don't allow your lack of a computer to EVER keep you from writing. EVER.

If you have a computer, you probably have writing software already installed as part of the package you bought. If you're not sure, ask a friend or associate with computer expertise to help you find out. If you do *not* have writing software, it is relatively inexpensive. Again, ask someone to help you determine what is best for you and your budget. And do not be afraid to ask for help to install this software and to show you how to actually use it. Do not let fear be a roadblock. You have not because you ask not.

If you have a computer, you have access to online dictionaries and thesauruses. If you do not, you can buy the actual books or borrow them from your local library. These two simple resources alone can save you valuable time and enhance your writing skills. If you need to know what something means, look it up. If you tend to use the same word over and over again, grab the thesaurus and find a new and synonymous word that gets your point across.

Once you begin writing you will discover that throughout the course of your day—even when driving to and from work—you will think of things you want to say in your book. Have some way of digitally recording your voice, like an inexpensive hand-held digital recorder or, duh, your smart phone's digital voice recording app. In that way, you do not even have to stop what you're doing necessarily. Just hit the record button, speak your idea, and then refer to it once you have time to actually insert that idea into your work. I do this ALL THE TIME—and so will you. This will give you peace in knowing that you will not forget that next great idea. Personally, I even keep something to write on next to my bed just in case I wake up in the night with a most brilliant idea. You may wish to do this as well.

We live in the most wonderful time. Technology advances have revolutionized the publishing industry and, thus, greatly impacted writing. If you do not have Internet access, go to your local library to use their free access. I utilize the Internet for research when writing, and so will you. All the wonderful quotes I am using for this book were found in mere seconds by simply typing the words "quotes about procrastination" or "quotes about having the right tools." Just don't be so consumed with research that you use all your writing time for frivolous Web surfing! Find what you need badly, then WRITE.

One of the best things I've ever done when writing a book is to send my daily written material—usually the entire chapter—via e-mail to trusted family and friends and writing associates. They give me honest feedback, and this helps inform and streamline my writing. If they tell me the writing is overwrought and needs to be simplified, I listen. If they tell me they do not understand a certain point, I try to make it clearer. If they see something I have not seen—a misquote or a fact I've gotten wrong—I make the proper correction. I learned a long time ago to trust those who love me enough to be honest with me, and it has enhanced my writing in so many ways. The biblical admonition to not cast one's pearls before swine makes so much sense to me now. I always wondered what that meant. Pigs will trample and defile what you put before them. So, what does one do with pearls? One takes them to those who will help care for and polish them! Do that with your writing, and do not take critique too personally. See it as an act of love rather than a personal affront. And always remember, it's your book. You can take or leave whatever your critics give you as feedback.

Another vital tool you will need is a backup system for your work. I use three different forms. I have two hard drives to which I back up my work. When I e-mail my friends the finished chapters for their review, I also send a copy to myself and save it in a special file my Internet provider offers. Another backup source is an online backup or cloud service set to backup all files daily. By backing up my work, I never have to worry that I've lost anything. Peace of mind is worth the effort you take to back up your work. And remember: BACK UP YOUR WORK DAILY!

Even though the last tool I will mention is not for everyone, it is worth mentioning. Some people simply do not have a gift of communicating that translates into their written prose. One way to look at this is to understand that not everyone who speaks with clarity writes with clarity. Not everyone who communicates well verbally communicates well in a written form. That is not a problem. Just because you do not write well does not mean you do not have a story to tell or something important to say. It just means you need to learn to play well with others.

If, from your writing, your feedback is "You just are not a well-spoken writer, but I know what you're trying to say," you may consider using a ghostwriter or a co-writer. This is what many of my songwriting friends do. Some may be good with writing melodies but are not adept at writing lyrics or vice versa. They do not allow this to hinder their writing, though. They simply reach out to other writers and ask if they would consider co-writing with them. They are still writers but have adapted their specific gifts in ways that enable them to still communicate their ideas musically. So it can be with written prose.

Join online writer groups. Search for authors who enjoy writing with or for others. Your ideas are still your ideas even when written by someone to whom you have communicated or dictated them. Basically, I am taking away all your excuses for not utilizing the tools at your immediate disposal!

Oh, I forgot to ask again. Have you written your outline yet? Just asking.

CHAPTER FIVE

✧

EDITING YOUR WORK

"So the writer who breeds more words than he needs, is making a chore for the reader who reads."
— Dr. Seuss

"If I can only write my memoir once, how do I edit it?"
— S. Kelley Harrell

"Writing without revising is the literary equivalent of waltzing gaily out of the house in your underwear."
—Patricia Fuller

As a new writer—or even, perhaps, as a more seasoned veteran—you will always write more than you need to. This is quite natural to the process. Part of the intrinsic nature of writing—at least from my estimation—is that each and every person who has ever existed, or ever will, longs to be known! We are relational beings whether we like it or not. Real life is lived in relationship with others. Think about that statement and then ponder the reality that should man and woman never walk in relationship to some degree, humankind would cease to exist! Relationship is key to life, and that translates into the need to write. After all, why do we write? If we are honest, wouldn't we all say that we—deep down in the depths of our soul—want others to know us? Whether you agree with that or not, we have to come to grips with that possibility—and use it to our advantage.

How do we do that? In my opinion, it boils down to seeing the big picture. We have what we hope and believe someone else will need, either in the form of personal memoirs or that next great entertaining novel. I write like I believe someone needs to hear what I have to say, and I tend to write a bit too much. Knowing that at some level my need to write is motivated by my need to be known, I capitalize on that reality and use it as an asset in this manner. I never forget that the other parties in this relationship—my readers—need to be known just as much as I do. This is simply part of my worldview and truly does benefit and help me self-edit. In other words, I never want to be a burden to my readers but desire above all else to help ease their burdens. It really is that simple for me.

The lifting of a burden can mean the difference between life and death for an individual. Something I share in a self-help/how-to book may trigger a response or plan of action he has needed in his own life that lightens his soul. Perhaps one of the characters in one of my fantasy novels might be dealing with an insurmountable burden and the way in which the character deals with that burden may cause a mental chain reaction that sends the reader into a level of freedom that was not anticipated, being able to identify with said character. Even while writing in an autobiographical tone—perhaps even more so then—I want to be as honest and intentional as possible in lifting the readers' burdens, without becoming overbearing. Such a worldview tends to permeate my writing and tends to help me self-edit in the process.

Even though self-editing is good for every writer and should be practiced with all diligence, do not make your self-edited work your final draft! You, as the writer, tend to see your own work through very rose-colored glasses. Such vision tends to be less than the needed objectivity. Being able to be objective about one's writing takes a lot of time and practice—and a lack of blatant self-preservation. You see, we are afraid that to have someone cut out certain words from our precious manuscript is somehow a personal assault on who we are! Nothing could be further from the truth! Having someone who is just as invested in your work—like a good editor—allows needed subjectivity into the mix. It brings balance and levelheadedness and always brings about a better final draft.

I will be honest with you. Since not all of my books have been picked up by traditional publishing imprints, I have gone through periods in my writing when I have self-published my work. In doing so, I have gone through seasons where cash flow was a very definite issue. On a couple of occasions, I released books that I have edited myself, only to have people begin to write back and tell me of mistakes they have found in both content, continuity, and grammar! How embarrassing! I wanted my writing to ease burdens, but it actually became such a burden to readers that they felt they needed to help *me*! That left me reminding myself that I never wanted to be a burden to my readers, so from that point on I decided I would use an editor!

Even though you may have cash flow issues like I once had, there is no reason you cannot find a good editor. One option I have used is to seek out a person who teaches writing or English. Once I have shared my initial need with a teacher and he feels he can help me, I ask if he will do a sample edit of one or two of my chapters. If I am impressed with the results, we negotiate a fee. Once that fee is determined, we talk about a workable schedule that is suitable to both of us. Some may prefer you send one chapter at a time while others may prefer the entire manuscript. Personally, I send my entire manuscript once it is done because by that point I have had a lot of feedback from friends and associates and have self-edited to the degree that I feel it is ready to go under the knife.

Having worked with several brutal editors during my association with traditional publishers, I have learned to not become so attached to my writing. If I truly do not want to burden my readers, then it stands to reason I must see my editors as those who will be vital to making sure that does not happen! And by the way, the word "brutal" in this context is a very GOOD thing. You want your editor to be able to help you cut away the excess—or to help you consider killing off your favorite character—or to help you learn there are other words besides "plethora" and "awesome" that you can use.

I love the Patricia Fuller quote: "Writing without revising is the literary equivalent of waltzing gaily out of the house in your underwear." No one wants to be that person. Having a capable editor who helps you craft the best manuscript possible will ensure you stay covered when you waltz out of the house!

When I encountered my first editor, we butted heads at first. I was not accustomed to having someone assault "my baby"— my precious, written self on paper—and I began to take it personally. It didn't take me long to realize she was honestly trying to help me and that, rather than fight her unnecessarily, I should get on board with the process and make the best book possible. That finished book and the subsequent companion volume both sold in excess of twelve thousand copies each before all was said and done.

While writing for another imprint a few years later, I faced similar issues with the man who was editing my manuscript.

This time, he actually wanted me to rewrite a chapter or two! How dare he tell me my precious baby needed to be rewritten! But I knew he was right in doing so. He even had the audacity—courage—to ask me to write an additional two chapters that I had not even considered, but I knew he was there to help my book be the best it could be—and I am so glad he did. That book was published in 2005 and continues to sell worldwide to this day!

What does one do if he cannot find someone to edit his book? This is what I would do. I typed in "independent editing services for writers" and came away with 86 million+ possibilities! You can also contact writers you follow on Facebook and Twitter and ask them if they know of any reputable freelance editors or editing services they would recommend. There really is no reason you cannot find someone to edit your work. The lack of having an editor in this moment does not give you the right to put your writing schedule on hiatus. You are a writer, so keep writing!

A great way to help ensure you have the best book possible is to write your manuscript with the attitude demonstrated in this quote from S. Kelley Harrell: "If I can only write my memoir once, how do I edit it?" What may seem desperately needed by you may appear as pedantic and off-putting to your reader. Write with economy of words. Become a wordsmith. Become a less-is-more thinker. Read the great writers of this generation. Listen to great lyricists of the day. You'll find that it is the "simply said" that grips your emotional heart and engages and nourishes your mind. It is the gentle flourish of a phrase well turned that turns your head and heart more than grandiosity of the verbose. See what I did there? I became a bit grandiose and verbose just to make a point. It is vital that you not be a burden to your readers but, rather, a burden lifter—even if you just scared their pants off in the previous chapter!

Oh, yeah. Forgot to ask. Have you written your outline yet?

"It is perfectly okay to write garbage—as long as you edit brilliantly."

—C. J. Cherryh

CHAPTER SIX

✧

THE JOY OF HARD WORK OR MAKING THE MUNDANE MAGICAL

"If you want to be comfortable, don't try to live your dreams."
— Emily Trinkaus

"To be no longer content to pick up what is floating on the surface of life, and to want only the pearls at the bottom of the sea, this is grace, welling up from deep inside."
— Eknath Easwaran

"If your dreams do not scare you, they are not big enough."
—Ellen Johnson Sirleaf

"What we hope ever to do with ease, we must first learn to do with diligence."
— Samuel Johnson

"Gardens are not made by singing 'Oh, how beautiful,' and sitting in the shade."
— Rudyard Kipling

"Amateurs look for inspiration; the rest of us just get up and go to work."
—Chuck Close

Once you have completed your book, gone through the editing process, and done your rewrites, you will want to know what the next step is—how to publish your book. While the purpose of this book is purely to inspire you to actually write your book, I completely understand your need to know the answer to that question. I will not belabor the points to follow but will merely give you as much information as you need to get started in the next phase of your journey—getting your book published. And this is why I began this chapter with the quotes concerning diligence and hard work—because that is exactly what will be required of you to get your book published.

> *"Nothing of great and lasting value is ever accomplished without hard work and diligence."*
> —Dennis Jernigan

Before we dive right into the depth of the bare necessities of getting your book published, you need to know the facts about the number of books published each year and how many of those books are self-published—and of those self-published titles, how many are sold on average by the common self-published author. According to Nick Morgan, "There are somewhere between 600,000 and 1,000,000 books published every year in the US alone, depending on which stats you believe. Many of those—perhaps as many as half or even more—are self-published. On average, they sell less than 250 copies each."

Yes, I know those numbers are staggering, to say the least. But you must remember that the population of the US is right around 318 million people as of this writing. What that means is there are a lot of fish in a very vast ocean of people who love to read books. The self-help/how-to industry (which includes books, seminars, life coaches, etc.) is a $2.5 billion industry! The fiction-reading world is a multibillion-dollar industry with an overabundance of genres and sub-genres! The nonfiction world is as wide and deep as there are people with stories to tell. Do not allow statistics to keep you from writing your book. If anything, let them inform you and help you decide upon the type of book and type of audience you are trying to reach.

Let us talk about the difference between traditional publishing and self-publishing. Traditional publishers generally take a manuscript, provide editing, and then have a marketing force to help them sell your book. This marketing force generally amounts to a huge platform from which to launch your book. Getting your book read by an editing board often means hiring a literary agent who will pitch your book to those traditional imprints. Generally, once your book has passed through the editing board's approval process, the author is given a monetary advance against the projected sales of that book. This can be anywhere from $1.00 to several million dollars, depending on the notoriety of the author and projected sales. Oh yeah, and that literary agent will get a small percentage of all your earnings from that book's sales from here to eternity (not that there's anything wrong with that, LOL!) And here's the kicker: traditional publishers generally do not take unsolicited (unasked-for) manuscripts, so you'll probably *have* to hire a literary agent to get your book in front of the right people. Because of relationships I have built through the years, I have been fortunate enough to have had several manuscripts asked for—but that is not the norm by any means.

With the advent of publishing technology, self-publishing or, as it's known in the industry, vanity publishing, has taken off! When I discovered self-publishing and print-on-demand publishing, it was as if my chains had been broken and my wings able to spread and I could finally fly free! Why? Because I could get my manuscript edited, formatted, and printed all by myself! And not only that, gone were the days when I had to buy multiple copies (usually hundreds at a pop to cut costs per unit) of my own books from my own traditional publishers and then warehouse said books before I could sell them through my own events. Print-on-demand meant I could have one book ordered and printed—and have it at my doorstep—and at a fraction of the cost of buying my own book from the traditional publishers I had used before! Now, when I am scheduled to speak at a conference or gathering, I can anticipate how many books I expect to sell at each event and have just that amount drop-shipped right to the venue where the event is being held! Freedom!

And don't get me started about eBooks! What a deal! In an article posted at www.pewinternet.org in April of 2012, we are told that 43 percent of Americans sixteen and older read at least one eBook or article during the previous year! By utilizing print-on-demand AND the self-publishing of eBooks, I can self-publish books and make them available in a fraction of the time it takes a traditional publisher and get my books out there working for me rather than sitting on the proverbial shelf waiting and hoping to have them published someday! Again, with the advent of digital technology, I was able to hire someone to create a website for me and post my books there in eBook form almost instantly! I also hired someone to prepare my books in the most-used eBook formats so they would be compatible with the likes of Kindle, Nook, and iPad readers. The sky is the limit!

Knowing that not every book I would write would need to be published by my traditional publishers, I quickly got on board with self-publishing. Because of the platform already in place through my music career and because of the advent of social media and the potential for an ever-broadening platform, I knew I could sell enough books to make money at this. Let's look at it this way. I could either write my books and let them sit around waiting for publishing and an eventual new income stream or I could write my books and actually publish them and have them making at least *something* for me! Let's see. Which sounds better to you? Making nothing or making something? Sitting on your gifts of entertaining people or actually putting your works out there and entertaining and helping people. I think you know the answer I chose!

Before I go on, let's talk about exactly what a platform is. I refer again to Nick Morgan's Forbes article. "What is a platform? It's getting enough people to care about you and your book, through social media, traditional media, word of mouth, bake sales—anyway you can. It's creating a community of people with a genuine interest in the idea you're putting forward. It's the way in which you create a strong brand around you and the book and get the world to pay attention." You probably have more of a platform than you realize. Let's just list a bit of the obvious. Do you have a family? An extended family? Do you have friends and coworkers, employees or business associates? Do you attend a church, or are you a member of the Rotary Club or some other organization? Are you a PTA member? I could go on and on. My point is this: you already have a platform regardless of what the "industry" says. How you use it—whether or not you use it—is entirely up to you.

I am not going to take the time to go into extra details about self-publishing, print-on-demand, or even publishing your book in general. My purpose with this chapter is to give you a heads-up about what to expect as far as having your book actually published. Again, the purpose of *this* book is to give you the basics you need—that kick in the butt—to get started writing that book you've always dreamed of writing. What kind of person are you? Do you see the glass half empty, easily daunted by the seemingly insurmountable mountain of the publishing world statistics, or are you a glass half full person who sees those same statistical mountains as an opportunity for freedom, adventure, and living out your dream?

What I have been trying to say is that getting your book published in any form is possible, but it will take diligence and hard work. Getting your book seen is a lot of hard work. Copyrighting your book is as simple as going to the official website of the US Copyright Office and registering your manuscript at www.copyright.gov. Editing your book is hard work. Formatting your book in eBook form is hard work. Writing your book is hard work. Building a platform is hard work. Selling your book is hard work. Dreams without hard work are fleeting wisps of air. Dreams coupled with hard work are realized in the most satisfying way. You stepped out of your comfort zone, put in the blood, sweat, and tears, and you have something to show for it. That which is worked for means more than that which was given to you on a silver platter. How can you fail when you have the right attitude? After all, the only failure in life is the man or woman who falls and just decides not to get back up. Just because you face occasional setbacks to writing and getting your book published does not equal failure. Just keep getting back up!

"A professional writer is an amateur who didn't quit."
—Richard Bach

Additional Resources for This Chapter

APE—How to Publish a Book: Author Publisher Entrepreneur by Guy Kawasaki and Shawn Welch
How I Sold 1 Million eBooks in 5 Months by John Locke

http://libraries.pewinternet.org/2012/04/04/the-rise-of-e-reading/
Suggested Blogs
http://www.chipmacgregor.com
http://www.writersdigest.com

Suggested Self-Publishing Companies
http://www.burkhartbooks.com
http://www.innovopublishing.com

Suggested Print-On-Demand Companies
www.lightningsource.com
http://www.bookmasters.com

CHAPTER SEVEN

✧

A NEW POINT OF VIEW

*"There is nothing significant in the world. It all depends on
the point of view."*
— Johann Wolfgang von Goethe

What Is Creativity?

Creativity, to me, is seeing life and its circumstances from a different perspective. One of the greatest disciplines I have ever practiced has been to learn to see my life and my surroundings and my experiences from someone else's point of view. To do so can prove to be one of the most productive means of unburdening your creative mind you may ever find in this life. To see tragedy from another person's perspective gives hope. To view hurtful moments from someone else's point of view brings maturity and grace. To see your place and purpose from not just your small place in the universe brings passion and joy. To practice creativity in this manner is to have a deeper understanding of why you are here on this planet in the first place. You *are* a creative person. There is no one else on earth that sees life from your particular point of view. Let's learn to release more of our identity and, in the process, release more of our creativity. That is who we are. You get the picture.

Here's something to think about before we go any further. Very often, we get so accustomed to viewing our world through our own eyes that we miss the joy of seeing the myriad of facets of life as displayed through the eyes or feelings of another. I believe this is because, often and without realizing we are doing so, we equate our comfort with creativity. To walk outside of our normal way of thinking or viewing the world is the equivalent of fear in our minds—and no one wants to walk in fear, right? But I believe that in order to become the best writer I can be, I must learn to step outside my comfort zone. What I have discovered is nothing close to fear. Outside that zone, I have come face-to-face with sheer wonder and amazement and joy and ecstasy and never once lost my own identity in the process. If you know who you are, there is nothing to fear as long as you walk outside your comfort zone with your feet planted on the rock of the security of knowing who you are! And that's freedom!

We are each given not only a unique point of view from which to process life but we are each given the ability to imagine worlds beyond our present reality. When I sat down to begin writing my first fantasy novel, I soon found myself immersed in a world of wonder where anything was possible. Not only that, but I discovered so many side trails weaving in and out of my road map that I actually felt like a boy seeing the Grand Canyon for the very first time! Soon, I began to think like each character—like each animal described, like an alien in a strange land might feel, like what I hoped my readers would feel as they took the journey with me! I never would have discovered any of that wonder had I been content to tell my story within my comfort zone.

To think strictly from your own point of view is to tell only a fraction of the story. It's like building a box around yourself and allowing nothing else in and nothing else out. What is in the box is all you get! Another way to look at not getting outside your own comfort zone would be to put yourself in that box and nail the lid shut—like a coffin! To tell your story from inside a coffin sounds horrid, right? And boring! Step outside your particular box and DREAM BIG! What does life look like from the mountaintop? What does life look like from a cliff midway down that mountainside? What does life look like in the valley? Same mountain—completely *different* and *valid* perspectives. GET OUTSIDE OF YOUR BOX! And the sooner, the better!

Following are some helpful tips to tapping into your identity as a creative being. They were gleaned from other writing I have done through the years, but I felt they were to be a vital part of this book in helping stir your imagination and passion to write. They have helped me for years. May they do the same for you.

"A stair not worn hollow by footsteps is, regarded from its own point of view, only a boring something made of wood."
—Franz Kafka

Refresh Yourself

Sometimes creativity means getting out of your regular routine. Have you considered taking a hike to help break the monotony of your job? Taking a hike may mean simply getting up and walking around the office. Such a walk may not seem too adventurous to you until you see that walk from another perspective. Take time to look at the people around you from a different point of view. What are their needs? What are their dreams? What would bless or benefit them today should you write for them? Our souls need refreshment. What brings refreshment to you? Clearing the mind does wonders. Need help doing that? Call a friend who is always encouraging. Don't have any friends like that? Call someone who needs encouragement and *you* be that friend. Take a gratitude break. Take just a few minutes and tell someone else how much they mean to you today. Get away from that computer or that knitting or that washing machine or that telephone for even five minutes and refocus on something that brings you joy— then apply that creativity to whatever creative outlet you may be pursuing or dreaming of writing about—and take notes!

> *"You never really understand a person until you consider things from his point of view. . . ."*
> —Harper Lee

Awaken Your Senses

Awakening the senses does not mean to do whatever feels good in a given moment. We were given senses to help us understand the world and the people around us. Our senses were given with, I believe, pure intentions in mind. Creative people are often attacked in the area of erotic awareness of our senses. There is a place for that. Learn to use your senses in a righteous and morally upright manner. How can we learn to do this? We must learn to see from another person's perspective. When we see a loved one or a coworker, what do we see? Learn to see them with compassionate eyes rather than eyes of judgment. When we hear someone speak, what do we hear? Do we listen beyond the surface and hear the meaning behind the sound, or are we too concerned with our own needs to hear from their perspective? We know that children need to be touched. Have you ever been with someone you knew could benefit from your touch? A gentle touch on the arm that says "I understand" or a pat on the back that says "Way to go!" Have you ever

58

wondered what an emotionally needy person might feel like to go untouched in life? Learn to taste and see from someone else's point of view.

"There are things known and there are things unknown, and in between are the doors of perception."
—Aldous Huxley

Color Outside the Lines

This is one of my favorite creativity boosters. I love it when people tell me things like: "You can't write a song that way. No one will ever sing it" or "You can't write a fantasy novel. You are a songwriter." Telling me I can't do something is like pushing me off a cliff. What may look like a fall for someone else looks like an opportunity for adventure and creativity to me. I should walk around with a placard that reads: "I'll show you!" Just because everyone does something one way doesn't mean it's the *only* way. Maybe there is something else for you to see you have not thought of before.

"What people in the world think of you is really none of your business."
—Martha Graham

Laugh at Yourself

I am convinced this is why I have children! Having an open and honest relationship with my children guarantees I will hear whenever I act in a hypocritical way. The older I get, the more joy I find in learning to laugh at myself—especially when I think I have it all together. The universe has an amazing way of reminding me of this fact! While driving down our country road with my children one day, one of my boys was talking with me about basketball. I was enthralled with the countryside around me. Just as my son was commenting about a certain player in the NBA, I was making a comment about the mockingbird that flew across the road in front of me. I was in Steve Irwin (*The Crocodile Hunter*) mode, being the smart, outdoorsman-expert dad I envisioned myself to be. My son's take on the moment? "Dad, you're scaring me. You're talking like a crazy person!" Rather than become upset at how my children did not see the importance of my "teaching moment," I saw the utter hilarity from my son's perspective and began to laugh. I am too old not to enjoy my life. This joy can only serve to enhance my creative abilities and insights. Humility really is key in learning to laugh at oneself.

"And those who were seen dancing were thought to be insane by those who could not hear the music."
—Friedrich Nietzsche

Go with What Moves You

When I think about the things that inspire me to be creative in my writing, I am always drawn toward inspiring stories. When I get down or distracted by the cares of my own life, I find it so useful to get my eyes directed somewhere else. My best creative times are when I focus on others—when I focus on meeting the needs of those around me—and when I focus on others who have overcome in some area of life. Reading about how Corrie Ten Boom survived and thrived through life in a Nazi prison camp birthed much power in my life to overcome and to be creative. I also was greatly inspired by the life of William Wallace and the movie *Braveheart*. I also greatly enjoy talking with people I consider overcomers—

people in my everyday life who have survived seemingly insurmountable odds of some sort and come out shining like gold. I DIG that! Whatever moves your heart, focus there for creative inspiration.

> *"The task is . . . not so much to see what no one has yet seen; but to think what nobody has yet thought, about that which everybody sees."*
> —Erwin Schrodinger

Create with Others in Mind

Hand in hand with what I just shared, I find that focusing on the needs of others—focusing on meeting the needs of others—inspires great and profound moments of creativity in my heart. As I write this, I have good friends who are facing death. The wife is in the last stages of her battle with cancer. The husband is watching his wife slip away. They told me of a dream that the husband had which has brought much comfort to their hearts. As I meditated on their circumstances and began to think about them, I wrote a song based on the dream. It has brought much comfort to their last days together. Just last night, the husband called and told me how much the song brought peace to their grieving hearts, and he gave me permission to share the song publicly. You cannot go wrong when focusing on meeting the needs of others. It tends to take one's eyes off of one's self and helps usher in massive amounts of creative thought—and takes my eyes off of my own burdens for a while!

> *"Look at everything as though you are seeing either for the first or last time, then your time on earth will be filled with glory."*
> —Betty Smith, *A Tree Grows in Brooklyn*

"Often it isn't the mountains ahead that wear you out, it's the little pebble in your shoe."
—Muhammad Ali

Explore Your Past from a Different Point of View

We must learn to live our lives in such a way as to not allow our past failures to dictate future success, or in this case, future creativity. So what do we do with our past? For one thing, we might as well stop trying to change our past! It simply cannot be done. Seek forgiveness where possible and then forgive yourself—and move on! So you were hurt. Do you want to stay a victim or become a victor over it? You *always* have a choice as to how you respond to *any* situation. You may not be able to change your circumstances, but you can certainly choose how you will respond and how you will let it affect who you are. Bitterness—unforgiveness—only holds you captive. We focus on our past as a means of remembering all we have overcome. This produces a grateful heart. Gratitude is a springboard into the deeper places of creativity. In the deep places of gratitude there is a wealth of creative power. Remember the past. Don't live there. Use your past like a rearview mirror, glancing back for a few seconds to help you gain your present bearings—but ALWAYS keep your eyes on the road ahead. Use what you've learned from your past. Be grateful for what you have, not what you don't have. Be grateful for what lies ahead. Don't fret over what you didn't accomplish in the past. Creativity waits for you in the place of gratitude.

"Distance lends enchantment to the view."
—Mark Twain

Give Yourself Deadlines

We have already touched on this previously, but it bears repeating. Procrastination is an enemy that debilitates our creative gifting. I find that I am more apt to carry out my plans if I give myself deadlines. I look ahead toward the goal I wish to reach and then begin to work out a plan backward toward the start. I give myself small, achievable goals and set those goals on a timetable. I make realistic goals and tell others about them. This helps hold me accountable to keep working towards the goal. Having these parameters or boundaries gives me so much peace of mind that creativity generally begins to flow as soon as I can see the dates placed on the calendar pages. It is as if I can already see the accomplished goal. This gives me much hope, and why put off hope? I always thrive when I have something to look forward to.

By the way, have you written your outline yet?

CHAPTER EIGHT

✧

CREATIVITY ON STEROIDS

"Life is either a daring adventure or nothing at all."
— Helen Keller, *The Open Door*

Be a Risk Taker

For some people, taking risks is the essence of life. I have climbed mountains and have walked on ledges with five thousand-foot drops on either side. I have explored caves where I followed a string to find my way back out. I have jumped out of an airplane at five thousand feet. I have gone scuba diving and swam with twelve reef sharks swimming around me for forty-five minutes. I have skied the north face at Crested Butte and the double diamonds at Breckenridge. I have sung in front of sixty thousand people. I have shared my story of redemption in honesty and battled the thoughts that are often the consequences of honesty. To take no risks is to close oneself off from life. If you risk nothing, you gain nothing. If you are afraid to risk loving someone else because you have been hurt in the past, you will not know love—because love requires relationship. Taking risks brings out the creativity I believe is placed in every living person.

I also believe the world is seeking visionary men and women who are willing to take the risks required to see goodness advanced. How do we overcome the fear of failure that often confronts us when risk is involved? We put on the truth. Truth leads to freedom. The first step toward truth always involves our honesty. The truth is that taking risks will always encourage others. Failing to reach a goal or failing at a task does not equal failure. Just ask Thomas Edison if the ten thousand failed attempts at inventing the lightbulb was worth the one success? Just ask Michael Jordan if all the missed baskets were worth the skill they helped build, which exalted him to the highest ranks in NBA history. In each case, both would say they had not failed at those missed attempts. Edison would contend he hadn't failed. He had simply found ten thousand ways to *not* make a lightbulb! Get a new perspective and be a risk taker!

"A ship is always safe at the shore—but that is NOT what it is built for."
—Albert Einstein

Dream Big

For years I heard people tell me my songs were too difficult for people to sing. My view was that people were more capable than we give them credit. Many told me I could not succeed in the music business unless I was in Nashville. My view was that I wanted my family to not need therapy someday—so I would focus on them and not worry so much about my career. In other words, I refused to sacrifice my children on the altar of success and fame and fortune. All I needed to do was to provide for them and to give them love—not to be famous! Did this lessen my dreams? No way. I continued to dream big even though the industry models all said I was crazy! What

I found was that people were after deep, meaty music and lyrics that spoke to their deep needs. I continued to dream of making recordings that would reach places around the world. I continued to write music and write books even without a publisher because my dream said that others would need what I had to share. My dreams were often loftier than my human eyes could see a way to!

I have learned that dreaming is merely the stepping-stone to living out my passions. At some point I must put feet to road and step into the area my dreams lead me, using what I have been given in that moment. I have learned to DO my dreams! If I can dream it, I can walk like I believe it! I write as if millions are going to sing my music or read my books. I write as if millions are going to be encouraged by the stories birthed from my life. I not only set goals toward those dreams, I actually begin to walk toward my dreams! I act as if they are really going to happen—even if people think I am crazy! I dream outside the lines. One of my favorite motivators is for people to tell me something cannot be done! Them's fightin' words to me! Dream big, then walk toward those dreams, and then step back and watch the creativity pour out of your heart and life. As you come face-to-face with an obstacle to your dreams, get a new perspective, which takes you around, under, over, or right through those very obstacles!

"An adventure is only an inconvenience rightly considered. An inconvenience is only an adventure wrongly considered."
—G. K. Chesterson

Be Open to Adventure

Adventure can be simpler than an African safari. For most of us, adventure can mean getting to and from the grocery store without our brains being frazzled from the chaos and/or road rage that sometimes goes with it! Adventure can mean getting alone with your wife and dreaming together about the future. Adventure might mean flying a kite with your kids (or by yourself!). Adventure may mean encouraging someone else when you feel you need encouragement yourself. Adventure is anything that takes our minds to a new place of joy and fulfillment that is out of the ordinary. What I have found through the years is that adventure, when seen from this perspective, actually becomes the norm. As with risk taking and dreaming, adventure puts us in the place where we find and wallow in creativity. In adventure, we also often realize the effect of having our minds cleared as we focus on something that may be very out of the ordinary. Creativity flows in those moments where we need to explore or where we simply enjoy life from a different point of view—even if we are stuck in traffic. No time need be wasted if life is seen as an adventure!

"Logic will get you from A to Z; imagination will get you everywhere."

—Albert Einstein

Imagine

Imagination is a gift. To use this gift, we must place ourselves in the midst of our dreams and goals. We must see ourselves at the end of our dreams even though we are not there yet! Do you desire victory in a certain area? Have you ever stopped to imagine what that would look like? Set goals according to these moments of imaginative creativity. One of the most powerful uses of imagination we have is to imagine what it would be like to be able to see the expanse of the entire universe without ever leaving the ground—to imagine what it would be like to be read by millions, to imagine or see myself as a writer! Much, if not all, creativity comes from using the gift of imagination. Just think about it—or better still, imagine if . . .

"Work is not always required. There is such a thing as sacred idleness."

—George MacDonald

Meditate

When I am speaking about meditation in the context of creativity, I am referring to the practice of mulling over an idea from every possible point of view until I have exhausted every facet of it. A great example or analogy of what I am trying to say can be found in the animal kingdom. Many ruminants have multiple digestive compartments. The cow, for instance, has four. Growing up on a farm I saw this firsthand on many occasions. A cow will take a mouth full of grass and swallow it, then bring it up and chew on it some more, then swallow, then bring it up for more chewing! Why? So it can gain all the nutrients possible from a single meal! So it is with meditation. We think about a specific idea—like the word *love*—and keep it in the forefront of our minds. From time to time throughout the course of thinking during the day, we can bring up the word again and again, each time looking at what the word means from a completely different point of view—like getting all the nutrients out of it that we can. If you don't already, meditate on ideas and step back and watch the creativity flow nonstop!

"If you can't manage yourself, you can't manage your time. Discipline and self-control are what get you on track to execute your plans by managing your time effectively!"

—Israelmore Ayivor

Be Disciplined

Plan creative time. Carve out even a few minutes every day. Follow your schedule—but be creative and flexible to the leadings of adventure all around you. Don't be afraid to say no. Others will fall in line to the way you do things—and they will learn to leave you alone. My own family knows that if I say I need to be alone that they are not to take it in a personal or hurtful way. They know Dad is in creative mode and that by giving me some alone time they are actually helping and taking part in that process. We teach people how to treat us. We must learn that urgent does not equal important. A disciple is a follower. We must follow when creativity calls. Following a daily plan is one of the surest ways to get the creative juices flowing.

"I have spent a good many years since—too many, I think—being ashamed about what I write. I think I was forty before I realized that almost every writer of fiction or poetry who has ever published a line has been accused by someone of wasting his or her God-given talent. If you write (or paint or dance or sculpt or sing, I suppose), someone will try to make you feel lousy about it, that's all."
—Stephen King, *On Writing: A Memoir of the Craft*

Fire Your Critics

I have enough people who are critical of my work. Heck, I'm more critical toward myself than I believe I should be! That being said, I have learned not to cast my pearls before swine. What do we do with pearls—those jewels of great value—like ideas, or songs, or dreams? In the "real" world, I would never place my pearls where a pig could trample on and ruin them.

I would take my pearls to someone who could help me polish and refine them! I spend time with those who encourage and welcome my dreams and visions. I don't have time to waste on the dream killers. I don't have the right to be overly judgmental of myself. Spend time with other dreamers, and encourage and polish their dreams and visions. Creativity is always the result. And fire your critics.

"Do more than belong: participate. Do more than care: help. Do more than believe: practice. Do more than be fair: be kind. Do more than forgive: forget. Do more than dream: work."
—William Arthur Ward

Surround Yourself with Life

Relationship requires giving and receiving. If my wife and I had never exchanged life by giving and receiving on a physical level, we would not have nine outrageously awesome children! Life is meant to be lived in relationship. To sequester ourselves away from others is to cut off our very life! Spend time encouraging friends. Spend time with your family. Share your creativity with others as a means of meeting their emotional, physical, or spiritual needs. Be a life giver. Surround yourself with life and watch the creativity come in floods you cannot even imagine!

"We've got facts," they say. But facts aren't everything; at least half the battle consists in how one makes use of them!"
—Fyodor Dostoyevskky, *Crime and Punishment*

Be a Napkin Writer

Creativity can come at the most inopportune times. I believe sometimes that my wife loves to watch me scramble around for something to write on when I get an idea and I am nowhere near my laptop! I have written songs on envelopes, magazine pages, napkins, and the back of my hand! No idea is a bad idea. Keep a folder of unfinished work and come back to it on a rainy day—or on a day when the inspiration isn't flowing so freely. Remember, nothing is wasted if we see life as an adventure—and are willing to write down those ideas on whatever is available.

> *"Weekends don't count unless you spend them doing something completely pointless."*
> —Bill Watterson

> *"Most of the brain's work is done while the brain's owner is ostensibly thinking about something else, so sometimes you have to deliberately find something else to think and talk about."*
> —Neal Stephenson, *Cryptonomicon*

Plan Time to Do Nothing

Take time to clear your head by doing absolutely nothing at all. I regularly request that my personal assistant schedule me time to do nothing. Some of my favorite mind clearing, "do-nothing" activities are getting my chainsaw out and heading to the woods, going fishing, wrestling with my boys, going to movies with my children, or giving myself permission to just sit and stare into space. How do I set myself up to really rest? I go fishing. This can be accomplished with someone else or accomplished all by my lonesome. I have also created a campground—in the woods on my property—where I can take a lawn chair, a cooler of refreshing man beverages, and a cigar and just make myself sit there for at least one hour. Rest can come more easily if we learn to take time to do nothing. Creativity is always enhanced by this type of refreshment. Give yourself permission to rest, then use it for—you guessed it—resting!

"Attraction and distraction are the two stumbling blocks that are essentially met en route in life's journey towards excellence."
—Anuj Somany

Reduce Distractions

As with risk taking, my motto is: "nothing ventured, nothing gained." What are your creative strongholds—those things that try to kill your creativity? If listening to the radio or watching TV takes away or limits your creativity, then get rid of or limit them. Name the strongholds or roadblocks in your creative life and deal with them. Use them for lofty purposes. If it's clutter, let it go. I periodically have my wife go through my stacks of stuff and throw away what I don't need. This helps clear the distractions those unfruitful piles can be. Learn to turn off other voices so you can hear more clearly. Finish tasks so they won't hinder your creativity. Unfinished tasks drain our minds as long as they are there staring at us. Don't be afraid to delegate. Creativity comes where the clutter is least.

"Tell me and I forget, teach me and I may remember, involve me and I learn."
—Benjamin Franklin

Invest Your Life in Others

Have you ever considered mentoring another person? Have you ever thought about the fact that what you write may benefit another human being's life? This always leads to creativity. Using our creative gifts to bless others is an endless well of creativity. I find more inspiration in this manner than in any other. You will find that the more you invest your life in others—the more you share what you've come to learn from your own experience—the more you will learn in the process! How is that not a fan to the flames of your creative soul?

"Sacrifice is a part of life. It's supposed to be. It's not something to regret. It's something to aspire to."
—Mitch Albom, *The Five People You Meet in Heaven*

Look Outwardly

Depression comes very often from intense inner focus. When we focus our energies inwardly, and have no outward outlet, we lose touch with creativity. How do I overcome a lack of creativity and, in turn, get out of that inward focus on "me"? I focus on the needs of others. I focus on others and how I can encourage them. I set my eyes on the finish line of my life. I do not keep my eyes focused on my past. It exists, but it does not rule my present or future creative energies. If I am on a creative journey (which life is), I do not get to where I am going by focusing intently on the image in my rearview mirror. That would be crazy. I look toward the horizon and keep my eyes on the journey, only glancing briefly in the mirror to remember how far I've already come. Humility and brokenness are the keys to creativity and right focus. Life is far too short to waste it on myself and my minuscule needs. I have chosen to tear down the idols I have erected to "me" and focus on bringing joy to those around me. And you know what the best part of that paradigm shift was? I found JOY and an endless source of creativity!

Outline, anyone?

CHAPTER NINE

$\diamond$

THERE'S ALWAYS MORE

I know, I know. I've already mentioned the thing about being careful to avoid using too many words, but in this case, I just want to help you expand your ability to step outside usual ways you think and help spur on your creativity. I promise, this is the last chapter on how to think outside your normal way of thinking. I just wanted to remind you that if you can dream it, you can set out on your journey to actually DO it!

"Aerodynamically the bumblebee shouldn't be able to fly, but the bumblebee doesn't know that so it goes on flying anyway."
—Mary Kay Ash

Don't Be Limited—Don't Limit Yourself

Who says you can't do anything you set your mind to? We are only limited by our willingness, or lack thereof, to work hard for the accomplishment of our dreams. You have been intrinsically gifted with a wealth of resources by which to accomplish that creativity. Literally, the sky is the limit. Never let circumstances dictate your creativity. Nothing is ever wasted if we learn to make lemonade out of the lemons life throws our way!

"Youth is happy because it has the capacity to see beauty.
Anyone who keeps the ability to see beauty never grows old."
—Franz Kafka

"The soul is healed by being with children."
—Fyodor Dostoyevsky

Play with Children

I have nine children—and nine new and unique points of view anytime I ask a question. And now I am having grandchildren—so the questions keep multiplying, joyfully so! One of the greatest joys of my life is simply playing with them. When they were little, I would help with the girls and their tea parties. The boys and I would wrestle (the girls too)! I got down on their level and saw from their perspectives. I still do that. I play with my children and learn a great deal about life. I learn to see life and situations as they do. Playing also brings joy. Joy brings laughter. Laughter is like a medicine for the soul. Be playful. Do you think God dreaded creating the earth? Or was He ecstatic and childlike in His glee? Think about it.

"Objectivity works to repel the attacks of critics, like a kind
of ethical pepper spray."
—Brooke Gladstone, *The Influencing Machine: Brooke*
Gladstone on the Media

Step Away from Your Project

In creating a recording of my music, it is not uncommon to listen to a song literally dozens and dozens of times in the creative process. So it is with reading my own writing again and again and again. Sometimes this leads to a numbness in my senses that leaves me without a gauge as to whether what I am hearing is in tune or not—the best performance or not. I have become too close to the project in those moments and need time away to refresh my senses. I take short breaks—a walk, lunch with a friend. And sometimes, I take several days off from the project. Rest your brain. Take time to cease from mental activity. Do something silly. Do things to help you laugh. Stepping away gives your creative resources and senses time to recharge.

> *"One of the great disadvantages of hurry is that it takes such a long time."*
> —G. K. Chesterton, *All Things Considered*

Don't Be in a Hurry

Don't let your desire to finish diminish the excellence of what you are creating. I have waited for over two years to complete two major recording projects. Talk about impatient! I have had to learn to wait. Sometimes in that waiting I have discovered there is more for me to say that needs to be added to the project. Sometimes I need to wait on the financial resources to complete a project. Sometimes I just need the perspective of time. Don't be afraid to wait. There are times when it is appropriate.

> *"It is not that I'm so smart. But I stay with the questions much longer."*
> —Albert Einstein

> *"True humility is not thinking less of yourself; it is thinking of yourself less."*
> —C. S. Lewis, *Mere Christianity*

Learn from Others

I love to watch or read the biographies of others. I find so much inspiration in the stories of great men and women who have been overcomers in life. There is a wealth of untapped treasure in the life stories of great men and women. Another great resource of creative inspiration is in talking with people who inspire you! You usually have not because you ask not. If you want to meet and talk with a favorite artist or writer, reach out to him. You'll never know if you never risk trying! And get ready to be filled with creativity in the process! It is the humble man who never grows too old or wise to learn.

"Preach the Gospel at all times, and when necessary, use words."
—Francis of Assisi

Show and Tell

Don't just talk about writing. Write. Whether you are religious or not, that quote attributed to St. Francis should speak volumes to all of us. In other words, live what you speak about doing rather than just speaking about what you one day *hope* to do. So many times I have written a new song—late at night—and called a couple of friends anyway! Even well after midnight! Sharing my creativity inspires more creativity. So often, the response of someone I share a song (or an inspiring chapter) with leads me to respond with another song (or chapter)! Share your creations with others. Use your creation as a blessing to others. Do not see this as a step of pride or codependence. See it as casting your pearls before those who will help you polish them!

"The features of character are carved out of adversity."
—Rick Barnett

"Thus, in a real sense, I am constantly writing autobiography, but I have to turn it into fiction in order to give it credibility."
—Katherine Paterson, *The Spying Heart: More Thoughts on Reading and Writing Books for Children*

Capture Your Past

Writing your life story can lead to a host of forgotten inspiration in your own life. Years ago I wrote my life story just as part of my own legacy to my children. This version of my story was not intended for public consumption but was meant as a legacy to my own family—to remind my parents of all I was grateful for and to challenge my children to have faith in the future. In the process, much creativity was unleashed in my life. In writing my story, I was able to document all I considered important and monumental in my life. Seeing how you overcame adversity in your life will serve to inspire others (like your children) to greater depths of courage in their own lives. In the process, you will be greatly encouraged by just how much God loves you—regardless of your past! In the first version of my autobiography, I wrote of all the good memories and relationships that helped shape me as I was growing up. In my second, currently released through a traditional publishing house, I wrote of all the hardships I endured that helped shape my identity. Both are meant to help and encourage people. Even if you never write your story for public viewing, I urge you to consider doing so as a legacy to those who will follow you. See it as a family heirloom, passed from one generation to the next. You will find healing, gratitude, and inspiration in the process. I guarantee it.

"We delight in the beauty of the butterfly, but rarely admit the changes it has gone through to achieve that beauty."
—Maya Angelou

Know Your Flow

Work when your creative juices flow the most freely. Utilize what works best for you, not what works best for others. I am a late night person. My wife is an early bird. We do not try to force ourselves to be creative in a way that actually works against our creativity. We give one another grace—and in the process a lot of creativity happens in our home.

"I dream my painting and I paint my dream."
—Vincent van Gogh

Creative Space

If we never give ourselves a place to create, chances are we will not be as assertive *to* create. Have a special place—no matter how small—where you can keep your creative tools handy. Fill that space with things that inspire you. My daughter keeps her oil paints in a huge plastic box she can take anywhere and set up as the mood requires. Another daughter has taken over a table in the barn where she has set up her torch for melting glass and creating exquisite beads. My wife has a rolling cart where she keeps all her jewelry-making supplies. I have a small one-room studio in a corner of my barn where I can hide away when necessary. The main creative space is between your ears. Set your mind at ease and you will have a constant creative space.

"If you were born without wings, do nothing to prevent them from growing."
—Coco Chanel

Celebrate the Small Things

You got the lawn mowed? Celebrate! An accomplishment is an accomplishment! Life is a creative journey, meant to be enjoyed! Take time to celebrate along the way. Share your joy with friends who appreciate your creativity. Share life with others.

"I want to live my life in such a way that when I get out of bed in the morning, the devil says, "Aw sh**, he's up!"
—Steve Maraboli, *Unapologetically You: Reflections on Life and the Human Experience*

Create with Purpose

Knowing I have a purpose and a destiny inspires me to do great things. Knowing I am needed goes a long way in producing a creative atmosphere in my mind. I create to encourage and bless others, regardless of whether I am writing to a self-help audience or to a fantasy-loving young person. I create to bless others. I create to let life flow from my heart as it was meant to; it will help keep me healthy!

"Is there any other way to be? I mean, this is it. This is my body, my soul; I gotta live with it. I'd better get comfortable. I plan on taking it for a long ride."
—Cecil Castelluccci, *Boy Proof*

Get Comfortable

When creating, wear something that makes you feel at ease. Some days I go to my studio in jeans and a tee shirt. Some days I feel like dressing up and going to the studio. I dress to enhance my creativity. If I feel good about myself (or if I don't), dressing a certain way can help me get into a proper frame of mind. I also keep a small refrigerator stocked with my favorite drink in the barn. I have a plentiful supply of my favorite pens and pencils. The lighting in my studio is such that I can lower the lights as the mood necessitates. I make myself feel comfortable so as to enhance my creativity. You can do the same with your creative space, no matter how small it may be.

"Every man takes the limits of his own field of vision for the limits of the world."
—Arthur Schopenhauer, *Studies in Pessimism: The Essays*

Stretch Yourself

Why should we place certain limits on ourselves? Who says you can't achieve something you have been inspired in your heart to do? Dare to do the impossible. Who says you can't have a worldwide readership living in a rural Oklahoma town where you raise nine children with your wife and the worst traffic jam you face in the day is the two or three cars whose drivers wave at you as you pass on your lazy country lane? I may live in the middle of nowhere, but thanks to technology, the extent of my limits knows no bounds. So it can be with you and your dream.

"If you're lonely when you're alone, you're in bad company."
—Jean-Paul Sartre

"Literature is the most agreeable way of ignoring life."
—Fernando Pessoa, *The Book of Disquiet*

"Solitude gives birth to the original in us, to beauty unfamiliar and perilous—to poetry. But also, it gives birth to the opposite: to the perverse, the illicit, the absurd."
—Thomas Mann, *Death in Venice and Other Tales*

Solitude

This has already been touched upon but bears saying one more time. Solitude restores the soul. Solitude—seclusion, isolation, privacy, retirement, retreat, hiding, concealment, reclusiveness, or withdrawal for a season—is a spiritual act that leads us to deep intimacy with our own souls and simultaneously reminds us how much we need others. It is meant for sheer enjoyment of one's senses. Even Jesus practiced solitude from time to time. So should we. What solitude is not? Solitude is NOT loneliness—alienation, aloofness, detachment, desolateness, or isolation from others. Loneliness is caused by withdrawal due to hurt or rejection or fear, which leads us away from relationship with others, which is a source of life and protection for us as creators.

I think you know by now what I think of creativity and how to see outside the box of your own perceptions and see through the eyes of other points of view. Utilize any or all of what I have shared if it informs and enhances your creativity. And get ready to put into practice what I've been preaching for the past few chapters—assuming your outline is done and ready to follow!

CHAPTER TEN

✧

LET'S BEGIN THE JOURNEY

"If you are going through hell, keep going."
— Winston Churchill

I have thoroughly enjoyed writing this book. Would you like to know why? Because I saw where I wanted to go, I stayed the course, and I finished in spite of the setbacks. Today is April 13. I began writing April 4. That's a mere six days. May I let you in on a little secret? The reason I began writing this book is because of my very first granddaughter. My daughter and her husband live in Sydney, Australia. My granddaughter was born on March 16, and I did not arrive until March 18. Not being due to leave until April 16, I had nearly a month to be grandpa to a newborn—meaning there was not much for me to do most of the time. Having read all the books I brought with me, I then began voraciously reading eBooks. Then my phone was stolen, leaving me with nothing to read. Bored out of my mind one day, my mind began to wonder how I could help someone else write a book—and the idea for this one was born.

"You may encounter many defeats, but you must not be defeated. In fact, it may be necessary to encounter the defeats,

so you can know who you are, what you can rise from, how
you can still come out of it."
—Maya Angelou

Rather than wait around for getting home to America to begin writing, I went ahead and wrote my outline. Rather than wait until I was in my favorite writing spot in my music room where I have a grand vista of the forest behind our home to inspire and impassion my words, I decided to waste no time—and began writing. One preface and nine chapters later, I pondered how I might end the book and keep to my word to keep it short and sweet and simple—and just as I was going to begin doing research online for this final chapter, the Internet connection went out. I can honestly say I was not discouraged by this new challenge, choosing to see the reprieve as an opportunity to rest up and refresh my mind for the trip home to America. Still, I wondered if I would truly finish the book as soon as I had challenged myself once my feet hit the ground back home, and I dove into my usual daily grind. In that moment, I could have given up at this seemingly, possibly fatal blow to the project, but I never have confused losing one battle with the end of the war.

"Never confuse a single defeat with a final defeat."
—F. Scott Fitzgerald

No sooner had I concluded that I would make the completion of this book a priority once home, the Internet came back into existence! That is why I decided to practice what I've been preaching and bring this tome to a fitting conclusion. And just what is that conclusion? You can either sit around hoping to write a book or you can actually begin writing your book! It really *is* that simple.

"It always seems impossible until it's done."
—Nelson Mandela

Let's go over the most basic needs of what it will require for you to write your book. And, while we're at it, let's take getting that book published off the table for now. If you're waiting around to have something published that you have not even written, how pointless is that? Let's do first things first! If you've gotten an idea for your book, complete the outline. If you've completed your outline, schedule time to write. If you've scheduled time to write, write during that time. When you have a chapter completed, send it to that small group of trusted friends who will help you polish it by giving you feedback—or simple, basic "atta-boys" or "atta-girls"!

"A wise man will make more opportunities than he finds."
—Francis Bacon, *The Essays*

Take it from me. Life has a way of trying to keep us down—from seeing the forest for the trees. Incapacitated and unable to work? Write during your down time. Do you have an hour before the kids get home from school? Take advantage of that hour and write something. Do you have a game of golf scheduled with the boys on Saturday? Play nine holes rather than eighteen and use those three or four hours you saved and write. Are there unseen or undiscovered blocks of time waiting for you to utilize? Remember, we make time for what are the real priorities of life. Don't waste another minute of time—unless you're whiling away the minutes WRITING something. Anything. Just write and watch the feeling of accomplishment spur you on to writing even more!

"Many of life's failures are people who did not realize how close they were to success when they gave up."
—Thomas Edison

Don't give me the excuse that "I don't want to write unless I have large blocks of unlimited time" because that is not the attitude of a writer and certainly not the attitude of one serious about honing his craft. Be resourceful! Use what you have! If you have five minutes, use five minutes. If you have five hours, use five hours. Just begin writing—and stop whining about the time you don't have—because, in reality, that's wasting valuable writing time!

"I am a slow walker, but I never walk back."
—Abraham Lincoln

Have you put dates and deadlines to those dates on your outline? If not, I suggest you do that—and then ask someone to help remind you to keep those deadlines. Be realistic, of course, but do not be afraid to assign small achievable goals to your writing schedule. One of my friends who is a writer has given me permission to ask her how her writing is going. And when I ask her, it's fun to watch her squirm if she hasn't put anything to the written page. We do not do this in order for me to chide her or to belittle her in any way. That style of accountability accomplishes nothing but hurt and discouragement—and that helps no one. My job is to encourage and to suggest ways around mental or scheduling roadblocks. While there is no hurry to completing a written work—urgent does not equal important to me—a sense of accomplishment is wind in anyone's sails. So, find someone to be the wind beneath your wings. By the way, my wife is my biggest cheerleader and encourager. She honestly makes me feel like I can accomplish ANYTHING.

She will be brutally honest with me but always leaves me feeling like I can climb that mountain or slay that giant when it comes to writing . . . to life. My hope is that you would find someone like that for your own life, whether a spouse or a friend or a fellow writer.

"Every strike brings me closer to the next home run."
—Babe Ruth

Please remember that you will have moments where you either don't achieve a certain goal or meet that deadline or feel that last chapter measures up. Starting over is always an option. Giving up is not! You and only you have the power to write your book. You and only you must choose how you will respond to the challenges I have made to you in this book. You and you alone have the power to make or waste your time. You and only you can resolve to sit down and begin writing. Do not equate writing a book with getting a book published. Live your dream and then give it to the publishers—and if the publishers out there reject your book, publish it yourself! No excuses. You can do this!

"Even if I knew that tomorrow the world would go to pieces, I would still plant my apple tree."
—Martin Luther

I began this book by writing my outline and then giving myself a one month in which to complete it. In spite of those few irritating circumstances I mentioned earlier, I came in three weeks under my deadline. Why? Because I simply began the journey—and one step led to the next step—and before I knew it, I had come to the end of the writing journey! I cannot urge you enough with these words. Simply begin the journey. Simply take that first step, and the next, and the next, and before you know it, you, too, will have a book to show for it!

If you have your inspiration, you are ready to begin . . .

If you have your outline, you are ready to begin . . .

If you have a laptop or paper and pen, you are ready to begin . . .

If you have time set aside to write, you are ready to begin . . .

If you had the time to read this book, you are ready and equipped to begin . . .

So what are you waiting for?

Begin . . .

"A professional writer is an amateur who didn't quit."
—Richard Bach

OTHER BOOKS BY DENNIS JERNIGAN

TP = Traditional Publisher
SP = Self-published
EB = eBook
AB = Audiobook
CD = Christian Devotional
SH = Self-help
ABG = Autobiographical
FN = Fantasy Novel

A Mystery of Majesty (Angel Award Winner) TP, EB, CD

This Is My Destiny TP, SP, CD

Help Me to Remember SP, SH

What Every Boy Should Know . . . What Every Man Wishes His Dad Had Told Him SP, CD

Fathers and Daughters . . . What Every Dad Should Know About Raising Girls SP, EB, CD

Giant Killers TP, EB, CD, ABG

A Worshiper's Guide to Creativity, Song Writing, and Ministry SP, SH

Victim to Victor EB, SH, CD

A Worshiper's Guide to the Holy Land SP, CD

Daily Devotions for Kingdom Seekers—Vol. I SP, CD

Daily Devotions for Kingdom Seekers—Vol. II SP, EB, CD

Daily Devotions for Kingdom Seekers—Vol. III SP, EB, CD

Daily Devotions for Kingdom Seekers—Vol. IV SP, EB, CD

Sing Over Me—Autobiography TP, EB, AB, ABG

The Chronicles of Bren: Book One: Captured TP, EB, FN

The Chronicles of Bren: Book Two: Sacrifice TP, SP, EB, FN

The Chronicles of Bren: Book Three: Generations TP, EB, AB

The Christmas Dream TP, EB, AB

Daddy's Song TP, EB, AB

A Thread of Hope TP, EB, AB

NOTES

PREFACE

1. Mr. Writerly blog. Writing entertainingly. "I have been successful probably because I have already realized that I knew nothing about writing and have merely tried to tell an interesting story entertainingly." Edgar Rice Burroughs.
https://stephenandrewbooks.wordpress.com/2015/06/05/writing-entertainingly-edgar-rice-burroughs-on-telling-interesting-stories/

2. Eastern Shores Writers' Association. Words to write by. David Brin. "If you have other things in your life—family, friend, good productive day work—these can interact with your writing and the sum will be all the richer."
http://www.easternshorewriters.org/on_writing.html

CHAPTER ONE: WHY WRITE A BOOK ON HOW TO WRITE A BOOK?

1. Goodreads. Ray Bradbury quotes. "Any man who keeps working is not a failure. He may not be a great writer, but if he applies the old-fashioned virtues of hard, constant labor, he'll eventually make some kind of career for himself as writer."
http://www.goodreads.com/quotes/231324-any-man-who-keeps-working-is-not-a-failure-he

CHAPTER TWO: WHERE DO I BEGIN?

1. Brainy Quote. Emile Zola quotes. "If you ask me what I came into this world to do, I will tell you: I came to live out loud."
   http://www.brainyquote.com/quotes/authors/e/emile_zola.html

2. Jazz Quotes. Charlie Parker, jazz great. "Master your instrument, master the music, and then forget all that . . . and just play."
   http://jazz-quotes.com/artist/charlie-parker/

3. Quotations Book. Quotes by Richard M. DeVos. "The only thing that stands between a man and what he wants from life is often merely the will to try it and the faith to believe that it is possible."
   http://quotationsbook.com/quote/4074/

4. "No journey begins without the first step" by Dennis Jernigan.

5. Quozio. A Spanish proverb. "If you build no castles in the air, you build no castles anywhere."
   http://quozio.com/quote/4836b0d4#!t=1033

CHAPTER THREE: THE ROAD MAP

1. Nicole Bienfang. Fix my life blueprint program. Kelli Jae Baeli, armchair detective. "Having no plan is like leaping off a precipice and trying to knit yourself a parachute on the way down."
   http://www.nicolebienfang.com/fix_my_life_blueprint_program

2. Brainy Quote. Abraham Lincoln quotes. "Give me six hours to chop down a tree and I will spend the first four sharpening the axe."
   http://www.brainyquote.com/quotes/quotes/a/abrahamlin109275.html

3. "Que Sera, Sera (Whatever Will Be, Will Be)," music by Jay Livingston; lyrics by Ray Evans; © Warner/Chappell Music, Inc., Universal Music Publishing Group, 1956.

CHAPTER FOUR: THE TOOLS OF THE TRADE

1. Goodreads. Stephen King quotes. "If you don't have the time to read, you don't have the time (or the tools) to write."
   http://www.goodreads.com/quotes/1404-if-you-don-t-have-time-to-read-you-don-t-have

2. Brainy Quote. George Herbert quotes. "Do not wait; the time will never be 'just right.' Start where you stand, and work with whatever tools you may have at your command, and better tools will be found as you go along."
   http://www.brainyquote.com/quotes/quotes/g/georgeherb119579.html

3. Brainy Quote. Washington Irving quotes. "One of the greatest and simplest tools for learning more and growing is doing more"
   http://www.brainyquote.com/quotes/quotes/w/washington120787.html

4. Brainy Quote. Don Marquis quotes. "Procrastination is the art of keeping up with yesterday." http://www.brainyquote.com/quotes/quotes/d/donmarquis107414.html

5. Brainy Quote. Mason Cooley quotes. "Procrastination makes easy things hard, hard things harder." http://www.brainyquote.com/quotes/quotes/m/masoncoole396387.html

6. Brainy Quote. Victor Kiam quotes. "Procrastination is opportunity's assassin." http://www.brainyquote.com/quotes/quotes/v/victorkiam107418.html

7. Brainy Quote. Edward Young quotes. "Procrastination is the thief of time." http://www.brainyquote.com/quotes/quotes/e/edwardyoun107424.html

CHAPTER FIVE: EDITING YOUR WORK

1. Goodreads. Dr. Seuss quotes. "So the writer who breeds more words than he needs, is making a chore for the reader who reads." http://www.goodreads.com/quotes/176857-so-the-writer-who-breeds-more-words-than-he-needs

2. Goodreads. S. Kelley Harrell quotes. "If I can only write my memoir once, how do I edit it?" http://www.goodreads.com/quotes/506611-if-i-can-only-write-my-memoir-once-how-do

3. Goodreads. Patricia Fuller quotes. "Writing without revising is the literary equivalent of waltzing gaily out of the house in your underwear."
http://www.goodreads.com/quotes/259758-writing-without-revising-is-the-literary-equivalent-of-waltzing-gaily

4. Goodreads. C. J. Cherryh quotes. "It is perfectly okay to write garbage—as long as you edit brilliantly."
http://www.goodreads.com/quotes/398754-it-is-perfectly-okay-to-write-garbage--as-long-as-you

CHAPTER SIX: THE JOY OF HARD WORK OR MAKING THE MUNDANE MAGICAL

1. Flickr. Emily Trinkaus. "If you want to be comfortable, don't try to live your dreams."
https://www.flickr.com/photos/63350375@N05/8644900309/

2. So Many Places. 25 more quotes about chasing your dreams. Eknath Easwaran. "To be no longer content to pick up what is floating on the surface of life, and to want only the pearls at the bottom of the sea, this is grace, welling up from deep inside."
http://www.so-many-places.com/2012/10/25-more-quotes-about-chasing-your-dreams/

3. Goodreads. Ellen Johnson Sirleaf quotes. "If your dreams do not scare you, they are not big enough."
http://www.goodreads.com/quotes/390551-if-your-dreams-do-not-scare-you-they-are-not

4. Goodreads. Samuel Johnson quotes. "What we hope ever to do with ease, we must first learn to do with diligence." http://www.goodreads.com/quotes/63061-what-we-hope-ever-to-do-with-ease-we-must

5. Brainy Quote. Rudyard Kipling quotes. "Gardens are not made by singing 'Oh, how beautiful,' and sitting in the shade." http://www.brainyquote.com/quotes/quotes/r/rudyardkip105296.html

6. Goodreads. Chuck Close quotes. "Amateurs look for inspiration; the rest of us just get up and go to work." http://www.goodreads.com/author/quotes/166434.Chuck_Close

7. "Nothing of great and lasting value is ever accomplished without hard work and diligence" by Dennis Jernigan

8. Public Words. Nick Morgan. Should you self-publish your book? http://publicwords.com/should-you-self-publish-your-book/

9. Brainy Quote. Richard Bach quotes. "A professional writer is an amateur who didn't quit." http://www.brainyquote.com/quotes/quotes/r/richardbac146140.html

CHAPTER SEVEN: A NEW POINT OF VIEW

1. Brainy Quote. Johann Wolfgang von Goethe quotes. "There is nothing significant in the world. It all depends on the point of view."

http://www.brainyquote.com/quotes/quotes/j/
johannwolf395609.html

2. IZ Quotes. Franz Kafka quote. "A stair not worn hollow
by footsteps is, regarded from its own point of view,
only a boring something made of wood."
http://izquotes.com/quote/98045

3. Goodreads. Harper Lee quotes. "You never really
understand a person until you consider things from his
point of view. . . ."
http://www.goodreads.com/quotes/25184-you-never-
really-understand-a-person-until-you-consider-things

4. Goodreads. Aldous Huxley quotes. "There are things
known and there are things unknown, and in between
are the doors of perception."
http://www.goodreads.com/quotes/50163-there-are-
things-known-and-there-are-things-unknown-and

5. Goodreads. Martha Graham quotes. "What people in
the world think of you is really none of your business."
http://www.goodreads.com/quotes/23499-what-
people-in-the-world-think-of-you-is-really

6. Goodreads. Friedrich Nietzsche quotes. "And those
who were seen dancing were thought to be insane by
those who could not hear the music."
http://www.goodreads.com/quotes/7887-and-those-
who-were-seen-dancing-were-thought-to-be

7. Goodreads. Erwin SchrÖdinger quotes. "The task is . . . not so much to see what no one has yet seen; but to think what nobody has yet thought, about that which everybody sees."
http://www.goodreads.com/quotes/13619-the-task-is-not-so-much-to-see-what-no-one

8. Goodreads. Betty Smith quotes. "Look at everything as though you are seeing either for the first or last time, then your time on earth will be filled with glory." From *A Tree Grows in Brooklyn*
http://www.goodreads.com/author/quotes/2327917.Betty_Smith

9. Goodreads. Muhammad Ali quotes. "Often it isn't the mountains ahead that wear you out, it's the little pebble in your shoe."
http://www.goodreads.com/quotes/371068-often-it-isn-t-the-mountains-ahead-that-wear-you-out

10. Goodreads. Mark Twain quotes. "Distance lends enchantment to the view."
http://www.goodreads.com/quotes/94270-distance-lends-enchantment-to-the-view

CHAPTER EIGHT: CREATIVITY ON STEROIDS

1. Goodreads. Helen Keller quotes. "Life is either a daring adventure or nothing at all." From *The Open Door*
http://www.goodreads.com/quotes/9605-life-is-either-a-daring-adventure-or-nothing-at-all

2. Goodreads. Albert Einstein quotes. "A ship is always safe at the shore—but that is NOT what it is built for."

http://www.goodreads.com/quotes/69315-a-ship-is-always-safe-at-the-shore---but

3. The Quotations Page. G. K. Chesterson. "An adventure is only an inconvenience rightly considered. An inconvenience is only an adventure wrongly considered."
http://www.quotationspage.com/quote/26278.html

4. Brainy Quote. Albert Einstein quotes. "Logic will get you from A to Z; imagination will get you everywhere."
http://www.brainyquote.com/quotes/quotes/a/alberteins121643.html

5. IZ Quotes. George MacDonald quote. "Work is not always required. There is such a thing as sacred idleness."
http://izquotes.com/quote/284566

6. Goodreads. Israelmore Ayivor quotes. "If you can't manage yourself, you can't manage your time. Discipline and self-control are what get you on track to execute your plans by managing your time effectively!"
http://www.goodreads.com/quotes/1145444-if-you-can-t-manage-yourself-you-can-t-manage-your-time

7. Goodreads. Stephen King quotes. "I have spent a good many years since—too many, I think—being ashamed about what I write. I think I was forty before I realized that almost every writer of fiction or poetry who has ever published a line has been accused by someone of wasting his or her God-given talent. If you write (or paint or dance or sculpt or sing, I suppose), someone

will try to make you feel lousy about it, that's all."
From *On Writing: A Memoir of the Craft*
http://www.goodreads.com/work/quotes/150292-on-writing-a-memoir-of-the-craft

8. Goodreads. William Arthur Ward quotes. "Do more than belong: participate. Do more than care: help. Do more than believe: practice. Do more than be fair: be kind. Do more than forgive: forget. Do more than dream: work."
http://www.goodreads.com/quotes/314867-do-more-than-belong-participate-do-more-than-care-help

9. Goodreads. Fyodor Dostoyevskky quotes. "'We've got facts,' they say. But facts aren't everything; at least half the battle consists in how one makes use of them!" From *Crime and Punishment*
http://www.goodreads.com/quotes/691313-we-ve-got-facts-they-say-but-facts-aren-t-everything-at

10. Welcome to the Quote Garden. Quotations about weekends. Bill Watterson. "Weekends don't count unless you spend them doing something completely pointless."
http://www.quotegarden.com/weekends.html

11. Goodreads. Neal Stephenson quotes. "Most of the brain's work is done while the brain's owner is ostensibly thinking about something else, so sometimes you have to deliberately find something else to think and talk about." From *Cryptonomicon*
http://www.goodreads.com/quotes/566413-most-of-the-brain-s-work-is-done-while-the-brain-s

12. Woo Themes Superstore. Anuj Somany. "Attraction and distraction are the two stumbling blocks that are essentially met en route in life's journey towards excellence."
http://quotes.pink/happiness/quote-14994/

13. Goodreads. Benjamin Franklin quotes. "Tell me and I forget, teach me and I may remember, involve me and I learn."
http://www.goodreads.com/quotes/21262-tell-me-and-i-forget-teach-me-and-i-may

14. Goodreads. Mitch Albom quotes. "Sacrifice is a part of life. It's supposed to be. It's not something to regret. It's something to aspire to." From *The Five People You Meet in Heaven*
http://www.goodreads.com/work/quotes/2561472-the-five-people-you-meet-in-heaven

CHAPTER NINE: THERE'S ALWAYS MORE

1. Brainy Quote. Mary Kay Ash quote. "Aerodynamically the bumblebee shouldn't be able to fly, but the bumblebee doesn't know that so it goes on flying anyway."
http://www.brainyquote.com/quotes/quotes/m/marykayash101496.html

2. Brainy Quote. Franz Kafka quote. "Youth is happy because it has the capacity to see beauty. Anyone who keeps the ability to see beauty never grows old."
http://www.brainyquote.com/quotes/quotes/f/franzkafka152018.html

3. Goodreads. Fyodor Dostoyevsky quotes. "The soul is healed by being with children." http://www.goodreads.com/quotes/80255-the-soul-is-healed-by-being-with-children

4. Goodreads. Brooke Gladstone quotes. "Objectivity works to repel the attacks of critics, like a kind of ethical pepper spray." From *The Influencing Machine: Brooke Gladstone on the Media* http://www.goodreads.com/author/show/4429313. Brooke_Gladstone

5. Goodreads. G. K. Chesterton quotes. "One of the great disadvantages of hurry is that it takes such a long time." From *All Things Considered* http://www.goodreads.com/quotes/262431-one-of-the-great-disadvantages-of-hurry-is-that-it

6. Goodreads. Albert Einstein quotes. "It is not that I'm so smart. But I stay with the questions much longer." http://www.goodreads.com/quotes/60259-it-is-not-that-i-m-so-smart-but-i-stay

7. Goodreads. C. S. Lewis quotes. "True humility is not thinking less of yourself; it is thinking of yourself less." From *Mere Christianity* http://www.goodreads.com/quotes/201236-true-humility-is-not-thinking-less-of-yourself-it-is

8. Brainy Quote. Francis of Assisi quote. "Preach the Gospel at all times, and when necessary, use words." http://www.brainyquote.com/quotes/quotes/f/francisofa109569.html

9. Goodreads. Rick Barnett quotes. "The features of character are carved out of adversity." http://www.goodreads.com/quotes/481229-the-features-of-character-are-carved-out-of-adversity

10. Goodreads. Katherine Paterson quotes. "Thus, in a real sense, I am constantly writing autobiography, but I have to turn it into fiction in order to give it credibility." From *The Spying Heart: More Thoughts on Reading and Writing Books for Children* http://www.goodreads.com/quotes/512179-thus-in-a-real-sense-i-am-constantly-writing-autobiography

11. Goodreads. Maya Angelou quotes. "We delight in the beauty of the butterfly, but rarely admit the changes it has gone through to achieve that beauty." http://www.goodreads.com/quotes/84834-we-delight-in-the-beauty-of-the-butterfly-but-rarely

12. Goodreads. Vincent van Gogh quotes. "I dream my painting and I paint my dream." http://www.goodreads.com/quotes/17974-i-dream-my-painting-and-i-paint-my-dream

13. Goodreads. Coco Chanel quotes. "If you were born without wings, do nothing to prevent them from growing." http://www.goodreads.com/quotes/51263-if-you-were-born-without-wings-do-nothing-to-prevent

14. Goodreads. Steve Maraboli quotes. "I want to live my life in such a way that when I get out of bed in the morning, the devil says, 'Aw sh**, he's up!'" From

Unapologetically You: Reflections on Life and the Human Experience
http://www.goodreads.com/quotes/tag/devil

15. Goodreads. Cecil Castelluccci quotes. "Is there any other way to be? I mean, this is it. This is my body, my soul; I gotta live with it. I'd better get comfortable. I plan on taking it for a long ride." From *Boy Proof*
http://www.goodreads.com/quotes/270508-is-there-any-other-way-to-be-i-mean-this

16. Goodreads. Arthur Schopenhauer quotes. "Every man takes the limits of his own field of vision for the limits of the world." From *Studies in Pessimism: The Essays*
http://www.goodreads.com/quotes/2194-every-man-takes-the-limits-of-his-own-field-of

17. Brainy Quote. Jean-Paul Sartre quote. "If you're lonely when you're alone, you're in bad company."
http://www.brainyquote.com/quotes/quotes/j/jeanpauls382887.html

18. Goodreads. Fernando Pessoa quotes. "Literature is the most agreeable way of ignoring life." From *The Book of Disquiet*
http://www.goodreads.com/author/quotes/7816.Fernando_Pessoa

19. IZ Quotes. Thomas Mann quote. "Solitude gives birth to the original in us, to beauty unfamiliar and perilous - to poetry. But also, it gives birth to the opposite: to the perverse, the illicit, the absurd." From *Death in Venice and Other Tales*
http://izquotes.com/quote/118907

CHAPTER TEN: LET'S BEGIN THE JOURNEY

1. Brainy Quote. Winston Churchill quote. "If you are going through hell, keep going." http://www.brainyquote.com/quotes/quotes/w/ winstonchu103788.html

2. Goodreads. Maya Angelou quotes. "You may encounter many defeats, but you must not be defeated. In fact, it may be necessary to encounter the defeats, so you can know who you are, what you can rise from, how you can still come out of it." http://www.goodreads.com/quotes/93512-you-may-encounter-many-defeats-but-you-must-not-be

3. Brainy Quote. F. Scott Fitzgerald quote. "Never confuse a single defeat with a final defeat." http://www.brainyquote.com/quotes/quotes/f/ fscottfit161657.html

4. Brainy Quote. Nelson Mandela quote. "It always seems impossible until it's done." http://www.brainyquote.com/quotes/quotes/n/ nelsonmand378967.html

5. IZ Quotes. Francis Bacon quote. "A wise man will make more opportunities than he finds." From *The Essays* http://izquotes.com/quote/9601

6. Brainy Quote. Thomas Edison quote. "Many of life's failures are people who did not realize how close they were to success when they gave up."

http://www.brainyquote.com/quotes/quotes/t/
thomasaed109004.html

7. Goodreads. Abraham Lincoln quotes. "I am a slow
   walker, but I never walk back."
   http://www.goodreads.com/quotes/6391-i-am-a-slow-
   walker-but-i-never-walk-back

8. Brainy Quote. Babe Ruth quote. "Every strike brings
   me closer to the next home run."
   http://www.brainyquote.com/quotes/quotes/b/
   baberuth125738.html

9. Brainy Quote. Martin Luther quote. "Even if I knew
   that tomorrow the world would go to pieces, I would
   still plant my apple tree."
   http://www.brainyquote.com/quotes/quotes/m/
   martinluth380369.html

10. Brainy Quote. Richard Bach quote. "A professional
    writer is an amateur who didn't quit."
    http://www.brainyquote.com/quotes/quotes/r/
    richardbac146140.html

ENJOY THESE INNOVO PUBLISHING TITLES

www.innovopublishing.com

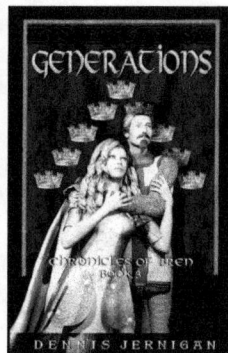

www.ingramcontent.com/pod-product-compliance
Lightning Source LLC
Chambersburg PA
CBHW071232290326
41931CB00037B/2680